PROSPECTS FOR AMERICAN POLITICS

ALFRED A. KNOPF   NEW YORK

1984 REVISITED

PROSPECTS FOR AMERICAN POLITICS

JK
271
,W66
WEST

Original Essays by
TODD GITLIN
GENE L. MASON
ROBERT T. NAKAMURA
MICHAEL P. LERNER
IRA KATZNELSON
FRANCES FOX PIVEN

edited by Robert Paul Wolff

UNIVERSITY OF MASSACHUSETTS, AMHERST

THIS IS A BORZOI BOOK
PUBLISHED BY ALFRED A. KNOPF, INC.

First Edition
987654321
Copyright © 1973
by Alfred A. Knopf, Inc.

Library of Congress Cataloging in Publication Data

Wolff, Robert Paul.
1984 revisited; prospects for American politics.
Includes bibliographical references.
1. United States—Politics and government—1945—
—Addresses, essays, lectures.   2. United States—Social
conditions—1945-   —Addresses, essays, lectures.
3. Radicalism—United States—Addresses, essays,
lectures.   I. Title.
JK271.W66   320.9'73'092   72–653
ISBN 0–394–48188–7
ISBN 0–394–31662–2 (textbk.)

Manufactured in the United States of America
Composed by Cherry Hill Composition, Pennsauken, N.J.
Printed and bound by Halliday Lithograph Corp.,
West Hanover, Mass.

CONTENTS

ROBERT PAUL WOLFF INTRODUCTION   3

TODD GITLIN THE FUTURE OF AN EFFUSION:
HOW YOUNG ACTIVISTS WILL GET TO 1984   11

GENE L. MASON THE FUTURE OF REPRESSION   41

ROBERT T. NAKAMURA CONGRESS CONFRONTS THE
PRESIDENCY   75

MICHAEL P. LERNER THE FUTURE OF THE TWO-PARTY
SYSTEM IN AMERICA   113

IRA KATZNELSON URBAN COUNTERREVOLUTION   139

FRANCES FOX PIVEN THE URBAN CRISIS: WHO GOT
WHAT AND WHY   165

1984 REVISITED

PROSPECTS FOR AMERICAN POLITICS

INTRODUCTION

Nothing is easier than to make accurate predictions in the field of politics. For example, as I write these words in June 1972, I can confidently predict that a presidential election will take place next November (since this book will not be published until after that time, you can all consult your memories to verify my prediction). What is more, I can predict with very nearly the same certainty that presidential elections will be held in November 1976, November 1980, and even in November 1984.

Not very impressive, you say. Any school child with an elementary knowledge of the American political system and the ability to count by fours can do the same. To be sure, the hidden presuppositions about the stability and continuity of American society would require a good deal of spelling out before the predictions could be certified as well grounded. Nevertheless, the real problem in forecasting the political future is never merely to say something true, but also to say something interesting.

Now as soon as we demand *interesting* predictions, we introduce an evaluative dimension that greatly complicates the business of forecasting. Many students of American politics would consider it importantly interesting—and not just an item of gossip—to know who will win the presidential elections of 1972, 1976, 1980, and 1984. For a variety of reasons (some of which are elegantly set forth in the contributions to this volume), I don't think it makes much difference which of the genuinely electable Democrats or Republicans actually makes it to the White House. The broad outlines of America's foreign and domestic policies have been continuous during the past quarter century, and none of the unsuccessful presidential candidates (including Adlai Stevenson and Barry Goldwater) would have altered those policies significantly had the election returns been different.

What do I mean when I say that Adlai Stevenson's policies would not have differed "significantly" from Dwight Eisenhower's in the 1950s; or that Hubert Humphrey's policies would have been substantially the same as Richard Nixon's in the late 1960s and early 1970s? Well, simply put, I mean that the distance between them is so small compared with the distance between both of them and myself, that from *my* evaluative standpoint they are virtually interchangeable. I have two Cairn terriers who have lived with me for the better part of ten years. To me, their personalities and appearances are as different as can be, but the first thing visitors always ask is, "How can you tell them apart?" I sometimes imagine that America-watchers in Russia or China, or even Great Britain, must have the same problem when they look at America's political leaders! As you read these essays, therefore, or any other attempts at prognostication, you must keep two questions before your mind: Are the predictions plausible, well grounded, supported by adequate evidence? and, Do they focus on what you consider to be the really important features of American society and politics in the coming decades?

How does a social scientist go about predicting the future? Indeed, how do any of us arrive at the predictions on which we base our choices and actions day by day? The question is, of course, too large for these introductory remarks, but it may help to distinguish *four* different ways in which we customarily predict the future.

The first way is simply to assume that some observed pattern of repeated events will continue in the future as it has in the past. As David Hume pointed out two centuries ago, much of our successful prediction relies upon assuming that the future will be like the past. Fire has felt hot to the touch before now, so we carefully avoid putting our hands too near it when next we encounter it. Even if we have no notion of the physics or chemistry of combustion, such "constant conjunctions of resembling instances," as Hume called them, can serve as rough guides to action and prediction. Despite the sophistication of the mathematical techniques used by political pollsters, election predictions frequently rest on nothing more than the assumption that patterns of past political behavior will continue unaltered in the future. For example, election analysts use the percentages of eligible voters who have actually voted in past elections as the basis for their forecasts of the likely proportion of new voters who will go to the polls in the next election. The remarkable accuracy of these predictions suggests the extent of our ability to foresee the future with even the simplest sort of evidence as a guide.

Nevertheless, as optimistic turkeys discover to their regret on Thanksgiving morning, a happy autumn of daily feedings cannot be extrapolated to a contented winter and spring. For most predictive purposes, something more is needed than mere "straight-line" projection of past trends.

Functional relationships, or the discovery that two distinct sets of phenomena vary in some regular way with regard to one another, are a second tool with which we predict the future. Samuel Lubell's detailed studies of precinct records have shown that beneath the surface swings of the so-called independent voter from party to party, we can find highly predictable correlations between voting behavior and such social indexes as race, religion, income, and ethnic background. Lubell's forecasts still rely on extrapolations from past patterns, but through the use of past correlations, he has been able to refine the accuracy of his predictions.

An entirely different method of prediction is used by all of us when we appeal to someone's intentions or purposes in order to forecast his behavior. If I know (in late spring 1972) that Richard Nixon wishes to be reelected to the presidency, I can predict that he will attempt to control the Republican Convention, that he will make speeches, raise money, try to placate indignant right-wingers, woo the new young voters, and so forth. My prediction is not based on an extrapolation from the behavior of past Republican incumbents. It is based on my imaginative reconstruction of the goal-oriented reasoning that I attribute to him insofar as I conceive him to be a rationally purposive agent. This sort of reconstruction, which the great philosopher of history R. G. Collingwood called "reenacting" the thought of the agent, is far and away the most common method for predicting the future. I use it when

I predict what my friends and acquaintances will do, and I use it when I predict what the actors in the political arena will do. Such "reenactments" can, of course, go wrong, so I must use all the available evidence to discover as accurately as I can the real intentions of the people whose behavior I wish to predict. For example, so long as I believe that the president and his advisors seek to insure that the Vietnamese people can determine their own political future, I will have no success whatever in predicting the actions of the U.S. government. But I may have more luck after I realize that one principal aim of presidential policy since the end of World War II has been to establish an American military presence in Southeast Asia to take the place of the French, the British, the Dutch, and the Japanese.

Simple extrapolations from past regularities, extrapolations based on past correlations, and the interpretations of purposes and intentions, all provide us with a vast corpus of reliable predictions in the realm of politics. Anyone who doubts that we really can predict the political future need only imagine how totally at sea a visitor from another planet would be if he had no information at all about our history, our patterns of behavior, or our psychological processes of deliberation and choice.

Nevertheless, these familiar modes of prediction frequently fail to give us answers to just the sorts of social and political questions we most want to ask. Consider once again the arena of presidential politics. Simple extrapolation tells me that unemployment, the cost of living, farm subsidies, and school integration will be issues in the next election, as they have been for some years now. Somewhat more complex correlations may tell me the functional relationships between farm subsidies, food prices, the cost of living, and welfare costs, thereby enabling me to predict the net-vote gains or losses that a presidential candidate will derive from a particular set of campaign promises. An analysis of the beliefs, biases, and goals of the candidates will tell me pretty accurately what their campaign strategies are likely to be. All this is genuine prediction and not to be scorned.

But suppose I want to know why there are so few real differences between the major party candidates, or why the political center in America is so far to the right of the political center in Great Britain, France, and Scandinavia? What if I want to know, as two of the authors in this volume do, whether there is any significant chance in the next generation for a major turn leftward in American politics? These questions require something other than extrapolation from past regularities in the analysis of the intentions of prominent individuals. I will need some systematic structural analysis of American society that will exhibit the lines of causal dependency among the many sectors of the economic and political systems. I will need a theory that tells me which factors are fundamental, which dependent or derivative. Most important of all, I will need some general account of the sources and forms of large-scale social change, so that I can explain and predict the great tidal shifts in American politics.

The first serious attempt to develop a theory of this sort for an entire national or international social system was, of course, Karl Marx's classic analysis of the rise, development, and eventual downfall of European industrial capitalism. Each element of Marx's account has been subjected to criticism both scholarly and polemical, and today not even those who call themselves Marxists would want to defend its every thesis. But in the century since *Das Kapital* appeared, nobody has done a better job of organizing the chaos of industrial society into a coherent theoretical framework. Marx tells us what is important in a social system (the system of control of the means of production) and what is secondary, derivative, and insignificant (the literature, art, philosophy, religion, and popular culture). He tells us where to look for the first signs of lasting, significant social change (in the shifting relationship of the several major economic classes to the system of production) and what can safely be assigned a minor role in our forecasts of the future (the personalities, beliefs, and arguments of the most prominent political figures). He shows us how to define the limits of the possible at a given stage of social development—which, in predicting the future, is as important as estimating the particular features of the probable. In short, Marx gives us a *method* for penetrating beneath the surface of social phenomena.

Marx's influence has spread so wide that his method of social analysis is used by serious social scientists of every political persuasion. For example, the recent analyses of the emergence of technical experts as a new class in advanced industrial society mirrors Marx's account of the rise of the capitalist entrepreneurs. Robert Heilbroner, Barrington Moore, Jr., and Seymour Melman are only a few of the American social scientists who have in recent years deployed the conceptual techniques of Marx to advantage in historical, political, or economic analysis.

This volume of essays by six of America's finest young social scientists is an attempt to get beneath the surface of American politics, to discern some of the underlying social structures, and thereby to achieve significance as well as accuracy in forecasting the next dozen years or so of our political life. It was my hope—though not part of the guiding notes that accompanied my invitation—that they might take steps toward achieving the sort of systematic theoretical understanding that is so lacking in most contemporary political analysis. The reader must judge their success for himself, but I can testify that my own understanding of American politics has been deepened by these essays. I cannot say I am heartened by the future that our six authors sketch, but I think I will at least be less surprised by future turns of events.

Before the contributors to this volume could set to work, we had to fix upon an appropriate time span across which they would attempt their projections. Forecasts of a year or two can be made with great accuracy, but that short a perspective allows of very little in the way of interesting prediction. On the other hand, extrapolations to the end of this century, which have lately come into vogue, leap over so much intervening time that they take on the look of Jules Verne's forecasts of technological miracles. Aiming at a span of roughly a decade, we stumbled upon the fateful year 1984. Our pessimistic associations with George Orwell's famous date unfortunately fit the general cast of our expectations for the future, and hence the title of this book, *1984 Revisited.*

The essays fall roughly into three areas, corresponding to the major divisions in the study of American politics. Todd Gitlin's piece on the prospects for the young activists of the 1960s as they approach middle age and Gene Mason's chilling look at the future of repression in America deal with what has come to be known as political culture. Robert T. Nakamura's examination of the shifting relationship between Congress and the presidency and Michael Lerner's harsh critique of the two-party system deal with aspects of the national political system. Finally, Ira Katznelson and Frances Fox Piven analyze

—and expose—the internal structure of the maelstrom of municipal politics.

Let me close these introductory remarks with a more personal word about the significance of the title of this volume. In Orwell's great novel, the true horror lies not in the physical tortures to which Winston Smith is subjected, nor even in the pathos of his eventual submission. Rather, as Orwell emphasizes again and again, it lies in the systematic destruction of the objective distinction between reality and unreality. Through the ceaseless retrospective rewriting of history, the party finally obliterates the structure of reality itself. "Hold fast to the truth!" may seem a feeble principle for times as troubled as ours, but it is the faith that scholars and social critics must live by. I would like to believe that each of the contributors to this volume is striving, in his own way, to separate the misleading appearances of the political surface from the underlying reality and, thereby, to help us all to hold fast to the truth.

TODD GITLIN

holds degrees from both Harvard University and the University of Michigan and is currently teaching at the New College of San Jose State College. He was active in Students for a Democratic Society in the mid-1960s and later as a community organizer. With Nanci Hollander he assembled *Uptown: Poor Whites in Chicago* (Harper & Row, 1970). He also edited *Campfires of the Resistance: Poetry from the Movement* (Bobbs-Merrill, 1971).

the future of an effusion: how young activists will get to 1984

"Anyone who was not a radical at twenty has missed something, and anyone who is still a radical at forty is a fool." Any number of establishmentarian cynics would like to take credit for this hoary proverb, for they gleefully anticipate that young radicals will come to terms, knuckle under, "grow up." To commentators in middle or old age who shared a youthful stint in radical politics, this version of the long view is as comforting as it is self-justifying. If radical activism is a passing phase rather than a lifework, the ex-radicals assure themselves they have lived the proper phases of life at the right time; having reached their accommodations with the society, they have not missed anything.

Meanwhile, the young activists insist that their radical commitments are lifelong, that as far ahead as they can see they will continue to be active enemies of the state. But the cynic, while self-serving, holds no monopoly on his prophecy, for indeed his prophecy is one of the activist's nightmares, the other side of the activist's confidence. Especially as his teens fade into his twenties and his twenties into his thirties, especially as his movement falters and he fails to see society change, the activist, perhaps in his late-night privacy, wonders whether he is condemned to live out the orderly oblivion to which the cynic has consigned him. The alacrity with which some young radicals are prone to accuse others of "selling out" and the degree to which the matter is considered to be purely volitional rather than circumstantial may be signs that all radicals are haunted, consciously or not, by the fear expressed in the cynic's taunt. Yet the future of young radicals is not simply a matter of individual choice, but a question bounded if not exhausted by considerations of social, political, and economic process, political organization, and ideology. The young radical makes his own history, but largely in conditions not of his own making. It is the task of this essay to explore the conditions that bear on the young activist's choices, the routes that will bring him to 1984, and the prospects for resolving the tension between what the heart wants and society allows.

I

The first possibility, of course, is that the young activists will disappear into the population as they grow older—that they will, in the cynic's words, "grow up." Four different arguments have been advanced in support of this prediction, none of which can stand up under close scrutiny.

There is first the view that the youth revolt[1] is basically generational or even oedipal: Young people in the sixties and early seventies are said to have been acting out of a rebellion against their parents. Whether defending their parents' values against their parents' practice or discarding their parents'

[1] This essay is concerned with white activists. While minority activists face many of the same choices, the social context is different, and therefore this discussion cannot pretend to encompass them.

values as well; whether rising up against the university administration, city hall, or the state, young activists have been "expressing" a desire to supplant their parents, and to realize in their own lives the power that their parents once possessed. Activism is therefore primarily cathartic, purging the young of unresolved family tensions and enabling them to grow into a more settled, accepting adulthood, or else self-destructive and suicidal, preventing adulthood and presaging psychosis and social damage.

This analysis is grossly inadequate and misleading. It cannot explain why youth activism arose in the sixties and not in the fifties, first in elite universities, then in other universities and colleges, finally in junior colleges and high schools. Nor can it account for the fact that hardly any radical activists have abandoned their radicalism, though, as we shall see, they have not always been able to sustain activity. The generational line of reasoning, whatever its limited usefulness in comprehending the energy of youth activism, fails to prove that activism is a passing phase of life.

A second and related argument, not nearly so cynical about the future of young activists, begins with studies of the origins of student activists in the mid-sixties in elite universities, which seemed to show that activists came disproportionately from upper-middle-class families that were liberal in outlook and had raised their children permissively. (In its vulgarized form, this argument blames Dr. Benjamin Spock for the student revolt.) Raised to have their own way, the children were prone to rebel against authorities who infringed on their prerogatives as their parents had not. But if activism had flowed mainly from upper-middle-class, permissive origins, then clearly the social base of the student movement would have been drastically limited. At some point the activists would have been isolated and thwarted within their own student bodies or within the elite institutions, and after graduation they would have remained isolated within society as a whole.

More recent data cast doubt on the permissive-family thesis. Richard Flacks and Milton Mankoff find significant differences between two "generations" of student activists at the University of Wisconsin—those active for three or more years before May 1968 and those not. The newer radicals tend to resemble the campus average—in class origins, academic discipline, academic performance, etc.—far more than did the veterans.

It is also obvious that the *institutions* in which student insurgency arises are more and more normal: Berkeley in 1964 and Columbia in 1968, but San Francisco State and Harvard in 1969, and Kent State, Jackson State, and hundreds of other schools in 1970. The spread of radical consciousness among youth in general, in the Army, among women, and in professions is further weight against the chance of isolation and, therefore, against the chance of absorption.

A third, familiar argument has it that student activism, whatever its social origins, finds its trigger in the monstrous concreteness of the Indochina war. End the war, so the argument goes, and the young will be defused. A few will persist in radical activity, but without widespread campus and off-campus approval for their bizarre and sectarian appeals they will collapse into factional impotence and easily be contained and neutralized.

No doubt the student movement was a tiny affair before the bombing of North Vietnam in February 1965. But there are difficulties in the argument that if they do not nullify it entirely, should at least temper the confidence with which it is offered. The longer the war continues, the more the activist is forced to conclude that the war is symptomatic of a larger madness. Common sense tells him that if the war were a mere mistake, an aberration, it could easily be ended. Since it is *not* easily ended, he comes to believe that something larger than the war is at stake: that American society needs the war. From there it is a short step to the realization that only some interests need the war, that their motives are imperialist, and that imperialism is the outer edge of capitalism as a social system. Examining and experiencing social institutions in this light, the activist concludes that the social order is unjust, oppressive, and corrupt—top to bottom. The war is a lens through which the true nature of American society is glimpsed. Even after the lens is removed, the meaning of that glimpse will linger.

Finally, it is argued that youth itself, the refuge and prerequisite of the youthful activist, is a temporary stage of life. Kenneth Keniston, not himself a cynic, has speculated that conditions in advanced industrial society have created a stage of life, "youth," extending between adolescence and "adulthood," during which larger and larger numbers of relatively affluent young people are free to elude the decisions of career and marriage that have absorbed their predecessors. Young radicals, along with various kinds of dropouts, adventurers, superannuated graduate students, and others, inhabit this interzone between adolescent self-discovery and "adult" commitment. Yet there is little doubt that the radical activist, with rare exception, is confronted with a fairly stark choice by twenty-five or thirty: He has either to find a way to sustain himself as a "professional" activist; or to join some institution, on some terms, in some spirit, that squares his political commitment with his personal needs; or, at least temporarily, to drop out of active politics as well as institutional life. "It seems likely," Keniston prophesied in 1967, "that many of these young men and women will in the next years face another crisis similar to the crisis that occurred at the end of their adolescences." The crisis is real and terrible.

But this argument must be considered carefully, for it may be misunderstood as implying that activism must end for most individuals as they "mature." That is, there may indeed be ways in which aging into orthodox work can be reconciled with radical activism, in styles that may in fact prove more enduring than the styles of youth. It may also be that the dropout syndrome is a prolongation of youth in a sense that Keniston could not anticipate; that it portends still other styles of activism. In other words, it is not at all clear that youth, in the sense of detachment from conventional definitions of adulthood, is merely a passing phase, nor that activism is the monopoly of the young. Perhaps "adulthood" is also in the process of being redefined. There is no sign whatsoever that young activists have resolved the end-of-youth crisis by *embracing* orthodox social and occupational identities. When activists do enter or resume academic or professional career trajectories, they do so for the most part uneasily, not wholeheartedly; they feel incomplete. They struggle not to accept the institutions' definitions of them but to formulate some other definition of the relationship—they are working simply for the money, or for some political reason, or because they do not know what else to do. They inhabit the institutions but do not belong to them.

The standard arguments, then, taken one at a time, do not persuade. There remains, though, the possibility that some of these arguments in combination, or some other factors, might drive activists back to the political-cultural paths beaten by their parents. This possibility does not seem very strong to me. Meanwhile, there is much positive evidence for the proposition that young activists are likely to stake out unprecedented futures.

The most conspicuous factor is that the young activists of the sixties and early seventies, unlike previous generations of radicals, by and large did not grow up in poverty. Quite the contrary: these are widely known as the children of affluence. Consequently, their drive toward conventional success, though alive in their socialization, loses its edge. At the same time, the young activists have experienced the costs of Americanized affluence and accommodation—suburban quiescence, the disintegration of authentic relationships, materialist competition, the fetishism of commodities, and the entire split-level nightmare. If there is anything unsteady in the activists' sense of themselves, and there is plenty, it is not their disaffection from upward mobility. This is not to say that the activists will necessarily reject affluence, though many do; but they will not pay nearly so high a price for it as their parents.

Perhaps as important is the fact that most of the young activists have experienced a set of life-changes usually lumped together as "youth culture," "counter-culture," or, more grandly, "the cultural revolution." Whereas previous generations of radicals generally shared the country's definitions of how to live, the new radicals for the most part try to separate themselves from the rest of the country, even to the point of submitting to ghettoization. Moreover, the young activists are not easily moved by appeals to nationalism, where earlier generations tended to drape themselves in the flag. All of this, of course, is trap as well as liberation; it presents enormous difficulties for a youth rebellion that wants to become a revolutionary movement, yet it also keeps activists from being incorporated into the American mainstream. The activist who does not want his own movement dominated by self-appointed or "democratic centralist" leaders will find it hard to adjust to the hierarchy of office, factory, university, or family.

Third, most of the young activists, however enamored of revolutionary leadership in Vietnam, China, and Cuba, are not beholden to it the way the American communists of the thirties were bound to Stalin. Even if Mme. Binh, Mao, and Fidel were Stalins, which they are not, and even if they were subsequently charged with crimes equivalent to Stalin's, which is unlikely, or even if, against all odds, they were guilty of an act so palpably foul as the crushing of the Hungarian revolt, it is very unlikely that American activists would be overwhelmingly crushed, demoralized, and discredited, or would go in search of a patriotic god to replace the god that failed, as so many American communists of the fifties did. Certainly the attitude of American activists toward foreign revolutionaries is admiring, often worshipful, but the relationship is much more complex and gnarled than that. There is a tentative, awkward, but growing understanding that however much we might admire the accomplishments and bravery of the Chinese, Vietnamese, and Cuban revolutionaries, the American condition requires a much different vision. And for all its enchantment with foreign revolutions, the American movement as a whole has no *organizational* attachment to them. Where illusionment is not so intense and salient, disillusionment is less likely and at the same time less devastating should it happen. Moreover, while many activists are in various degrees unhappy and even bitter about recent developments in the movement, we have been singularly spared the agonies of recantation and recrimination that have served earlier radicals as prologues to incorporation. Of course, the movement could shield its vulnerability if it could agree on the special requirements of an American revolution, on a theory of change to suit the requirements of a society which needs revolution not to achieve industrialization but to transcend it.

Fourth, the Indochinese war is the defining generational event for the young activists of the sixties and early seventies. It divides them into two distinct subgenerations: those who began their political careers before 1965 and those who began afterward. The first subgeneration came into political awareness in a time of political opening—the Cuban revolution, the civil rights movement, the New Frontier. Their prime political mood was *radical disappointment*—the sense that American liberal forces were failing *by their own lights*. The second subgeneration grew up with far fewer liberal illusions. The twenty-year-old activist of 1971 has not known the promise of liberalism, only the genocidal payoff; he has lived with the war since his early adolescence. He is not so much disappointed or disillusioned as enraged. He is less beholden to his elders, and his view of the world is not tinged with so much nostalgia for the liberal dream. Moreover, he has far more choice in life style and political work than did the earlier subgeneration: Revolution seems to him a more credible proposition. He feels something like a *revolutionary imperative.* The newer activists are more seasoned in implacability than the older ones; they are less and less likely to find occupational, sexual, or political peace within the standard package of career, marriage, and political orthodoxy. Since, as we shall see, even the older activists have refused to settle into conventional identities, it stands to reason that the newer activists will prove at least as enduring.

Finally, hindsight indicates that earlier American radicals melted themselves back into the American crucible because they simply had no other choice—either economic or cultural. Conditions in the last third of the twentieth century are much different. There are ways to live in the margins of the political economy that did not exist thirty years ago. There is a growing counter-culture that affords some, though not nearly enough, sustenance—water in which fish may swim. There are definitions of radical work—primarily in the professions—that eluded movements whose historical chips were placed exclusively on the industrial proletariat: movements that preceded the rise in the economic importance of educated labor. So there is little reason to believe that the youth activists of today are headed back to the political cultural paths beaten by their parents.

It seems truistic to point out that the future begins now, but the truism is helpful in making projections. For at this moment, in the spring of 1972, the young activists of the early and mid-sixties have already occupied the first tiers of their futures, and they prefigure at least some possibilities and obstacles that will loom by 1984. Using the present as intimation of the future, then, it seems to me that there are two rough models for the future of youth activists: call them minimum and maximum futures.

II

In the minimum future, aging activists will settle, easily or uneasily, into one of three styles of life and political work. Some will shuttle back and forth from one to another, but the roles themselves are rather distinct.

1. *"Professional" Radicals.* A minority will continue to be "professional" activists without career portfolios: They will plant themselves in youth ghettos as experienced hands; or in factories, neighborhoods, and fields as organizers of radical unions, caucuses, or community organizations; or in the various offices of radical groups. Some will combine particular quasi-professional skills with their radical work—for instance, the thousands of activists who are now occupied with the production and distribution of hundreds of radical newspapers and films—but their primary identity will come from a sense of belonging to a movement larger and more salient to them than their particular roles.[2]

The hazards of professional activism flow directly from the main advantages—single-minded concentration on political work and freedom from institutional constraints. In the face of repression and in the absence of visible social change, the professional is thrown back on his inner stability and on the support of comrades. Especially in the absence of an organized movement, which can help establish ideological clarity, work priorities, and a sense of national direction, he must resort to the homogeneity of a small work- or living-collective. He is especially vulnerable to despair, isolation, and feelings of impermanence, all built into his sense of political calling, which may be only partially countered by ideological or moral certitude. Perhaps more devastating, though, are the political consequences of the style of work which professionals have gravitated toward. For many, active political work is episodic and *ad hoc:* preparation for this demonstration, that conference, the other electoral campaign. When the event passes, the professional may resort to the role of free-floating celebrity, or he may be again confronted with the specialness of his social role and with his need somehow to engage the lives of people lodged in orthodox roles. If he submits to being a celebrity, he is easily incorporated, substituting media recognition for political base and finally losing touch with political

---

[2] The media-producing radicals are something of a special case. Even though their work is almost always divorced from a concrete insurgent strategy, and is therefore unsystematic and noncumulative, it is more or less full-time work that identifies wholeheartedly with the movement and that at least claims political relevance. But at the same time the products are hermetically sealed within the youth enclaves and are probably a dead end.

reality and with the people for whom he claims to be spokesman. If, on the other hand, he chooses the painful and thank-
less task of leader, organizer, and mobilizer of movement
events, he must be able to practice skillfully the old-fashioned
and, one suspects, waning political arts of alliance and nego-
tiation, to withstand the deep resentments of an antiauthoritarian movement, and to find a delicate balance between
initiative and responsiveness. The difficulty of this role is
starkly revealed by the fact that only a handful have pursued
it for more than a few years.

The professional's distinctness from the people whom he
wants to activate, juxtaposed to his need to mobilize those
very people, leads to elitism. The elitist danger is especially
grave when the professional is working with people who are
"beneath" him in class, political culture, or ideological stance,
for then he is tempted to usurp the privilege of leading them
to the promised land.

But even equipped with a conception of organizing as
catalysis rather than *indispensable leadership,* the professional
who is not crystal-clear about his own motives, aware of how
his experience diverges from that of The Others and creates
in him a need to dominate, is likely to succumb to traditional
"vanguard" roles which are either ineffectual or oppressive.
This risk is accentuated for those radicals working in the small
sects which are the residue of the mass student movement of
the sixties, for they firmly believe in their own special possession of the key to revolutionary success, namely one or
another variant of Marxism-Leninism. Huddled together for
security ("correctness") in the face of a hostile reality, unable
to assess their work and grow because ironclad ideology
encapsulates them from political reality, these sectarian remnants are probably doomed to lives of fratricide, self-mystification, irrelevant politics and political irrelevance. But even
those professionals who do not succumb to one or another
prepackaged political identity, who recognize that twentieth-
century America is not nineteenth-century Russia or twentieth-
century China or Cuba, and that America requires an unprecedented revolution, are likely to suffer both psychologically and
politically in the absence of an organized movement that can
lend substance and reality-test to their dreams. The professional role would be much easier to sustain if it were infused

with a clear sense of political objective or revolutionary trajectory, now lacking.

Professional activism has not been a satisfying choice for the young activists of the sixties, nor has it been a common one. But conceivably some of the obstacles will dissipate in the next few years. Newer activists differ from the older ones in important ways. They have a physical community, the youth enclave, to fall back on and derive some strength. The enclave is enclosure as well as home, but at least it is available. Rather early in their lives they have become accustomed to integrating political concerns and life style; they might succeed in working out more open and egalitarian relationships. And having thrown off at least the trappings of the Protestant ethic, they might be less tempted by orthodox careers. All in all they seem more likely to find routes to professional activism, especially the women, who have come to understand that their "personal" troubles have political dimensions and that they can integrate their liberation from both in a separate women's movement. But many younger men, prompted by the women's movement, also seem to have an enlarged sensitivity to problems of work relationships and seem to stand a good chance of moderating the competitiveness and *machismo* that tied earlier activists in knots.

2. *Radical Professionals.* Still more likely, and probably more auspicious politically, is the choice to take up an orthodox career, and then to use one's professional skill and experience as a base for political activism. Young doctors, lawyers, and academics in some disciplines, many of them veterans of the activist struggles of the sixties, have been able to form outward-facing political groups that have become major presences within their professions. Radicals like myself, who wondered skeptically and self-righteously in 1967 whether "radical in the professions" was not a contradiction in terms —because of the relative comfort, the hierarchy of the professional-client relationship, and the institutional limits within which it takes place—have had to take a second look. In fact, these clusters and organizations have been able to undertake three terribly important projects. First, they have made their own demands and bolstered clients' demands for fuller and cheaper services responsible to clients: thus, doctors give aid to community demands for free clinics and

campaign for abortion reform and academics support student protests. Second, they have challenged the reactionary practices of the rest of the profession by undertaking serious analysis of the profession's place in the social system, by challenging corporate domination and the careerist ethos, by articulating a radical alternative, and, crucially, by erecting models of nonoppressive radical practice against which colleagues and apprentices can measure the profession as a whole. And third, they have set up counter-institutions and examples of nonhierarchical, people-centered work, both within and outside the main institutions of the professions: thus free medical clinics, law communes that take their political direction from clients, and public-service law firms.

No doubt this work is flawed by the pressure of the institutional settings themselves and by the temptation to lapse into the privilege of professional status. It is certainly limited by the fact that often the radical professionals are considerably more activist than the clients and communities with whom they would like to create a new relationship and join forces. And, at the same time, radical professionalism has thus far been limited to the "upper" professions—sometimes city planning, architecture, religion, and journalism as well as medicine, law, and college teaching—and has not really penetrated to the "lower" and more proletarianized: public-school teaching, engineering, nursing, and social work. This is not surprising, considering the elite origins and elite university training of much of the early sixties student movement. But inasmuch as the class base of student activism has widened since, one would expect to find a corresponding radicalization within the "lower" professions and even more proletarianized white-collar levels in the coming years—even in the offices of the state and the corporations themselves. Their political effect would be marked, as these professions grow in size and economic importance proportionate to the work force as a whole.

There are advantages to the radical professional's style of work. Unlike the professional radical who tries (and usually fails) to organize people who in class and culture are unlike himself, the radical professional is oriented toward both colleagues and clients. Sharing with his colleagues class and culture, some common experience, and often a common victimization within the institutions of employment, the radical professional is more easily able to engage others and less likely to move out when the going gets rough. Moreover, his political work is less likely than the professional radical's to be merely episodic. He is often in daily, unforced contact with both colleagues and clients; he does not have to knock on a strange door and explain his presence in order to engage someone in conversation.

Yet there are limits to radical professionalism. Obviously, the radical professionals are vulnerable to being fired, while their standards of living and dependence on career-identity drive up the price. In the absence of mass radical movement at every level of the society, activism within the professions can become cloistered, closed in on itself: an interesting clamor that does not touch the heart of anyone else's life. Isolated from newer radicals and from professional activists, the radical professional may find that attentiveness to his own work keeps him from participating in a larger movement. Meanwhile, the productive core of the political economy lies essentially untouched. Theorists of the "new working class" of white-collar workers, professionals, technicians, and managers, who speculate that uprisings of these groups could expropriate the most advanced sectors of the economy, have yet to explain why the specialist/engineers and technicians have not mobilized, when the generalist/humanists and older professions are already in motion. Yet at a point that is at least conceivable, when engineers refuse to design a new missile, architects refuse to design a new downtown office building, and teachers refuse to use the textbooks, radical professionalism will be formidable.

3. *"Role Your Own."* The categories of professional radical and radical professional do not and will not exhaust the future of young activists. The last few years have seen the opening up of roles—or, perhaps, nonroles—which hardly anyone had anticipated. Unable to sustain the breakneck pace, specialness, and insecurity of the full-time activist and unwilling to rejoin the career trajectories long abandoned (not so much from fear of "selling out" as from distaste for fixed, oppressive, or inexpressive roles), a small but growing number of movement veterans have dropped out—out of active political work, out of careers, out of school, and often out of the cities. A number of factors have intersected to produce this unexpected fallout: simple battle fatigue, which is never simple, but which expresses anxieties that are compounded by dedication and a sense of

obligation or guilt, and that emerge with a vengeance in the heat of activity; the sheer stress and pain of movement work over a long period of time (such feelings are often unrewarded by social change or are unable to absorb the progress already made); the fragmentation, fratricide, posturing, male chauvinism, and self-mystification of the movement, and the sense that movement activity has become "unreal," frozen or theatrical; the need for time to recover or uncover a self left long untended in the course of political work, to intensify person-to-person relationships, and to absorb and make sense of the overpowering experience of the past. The counter-culture and the wilderness, hybridized in the rural commune, become a natural resting place. Other activists do not leave the cities or political work but live by odd—often manual—jobs, which leave them time to engage in an occasional political project. Or they get by with part-time teaching or writing and cannot find any other congenial political work.

What both types of dropouts—total and partial—have in common is that they "role their own"—in Keniston's sense they attempt to prolong "youth" without embracing clear-cut definitions. They also, in almost every case, remain definitely radical—unlike the apostates of previous generations, they do not revoke their general political outlook; they undertake nothing so dramatic as a shift from pro-Soviet to anti-Soviet, though of course they do revise their ideas. Their experiment is primarily with life style, and they have not rejoined the mainstream. Some of these dropouts are forward-looking, absorbed in living a life instead of measuring the distance to the revolutionary horizon; others are back-glancing, somewhat cynical, and, for at least a while, in some sense of the term, "burned out."[3]

In what sense are these nonroles "political"? It is easy to say how they are not—the dropouts are not animated by strategy or by head-on engagement in the process of changing

---

[3] According to a Cuban informant, twenty-sixth-of-July militants experienced two periods in which "burn-outs" (the Spanish word is *quemarse*, "to burn oneself") were common: between the (unsuccessful) assault on Moncade barracks in 1953 and the landing of the *Granma* in 1956 and after the seizure of power in 1959. The first roughly corresponds to the American present; the second may indicate sheer exhaustion from a job well done, which at this distance sounds almost pleasant.

social policy and institutions; they are not much interested in organizing anyone other than themselves. And there is an aspect of some nonroles that is neither "political" nor "apolitical," but simply necessary for psychic survival— decompression, retreat, and recovery. But these facts are not the whole story. The recovery of self and the testing of new possibilities in work and love have an exemplary aspect—not the naïve utopianism according to which a revolution of attitudes will spring from spontaneous emulation of the new lives, but the principle that the new life is *itself* a test of revolutionary attitudes, a way of validating beliefs ("testing theory by practice") on a scale that makes sense. For activists who discover that their political goals and rhetoric have outdistanced their intuitive sense of their own place in the process of making change, or who discover that their previous political roles were either negligible or harmful, the nonrole is not just necessary recovery, it is a prelude to any future engagement.

On the face of it such a position does not seem permanent, yet it is hard to predict exactly what would terminate the nonrole and open into new possibilities. One terminus to the dropout life, a prospect not to be dismissed lightly, might be economic stagnation that crushes its economic base: marginal and part-time jobs dry up, and welfare is made much more restrictive. Rural communes might be able to sustain themselves nonetheless, but some dropout radicals would reenter the ranks of the unemployed, and they might be tempted willy-nilly to resume identities as professional radicals or radical professionals. A second possibility is that an organized movement might reemerge with which the dropouts could identify comfortably, because it offers plausible expectations that political work might make a political difference, or because it is open in style, or because it exudes ideology that squares with and makes sense of actual experience. Third, it is conceivable that part-time work, whether as teacher or waitress, might engender the drive to organize on the job; but this would be scattered and unconcerted. Whatever the ways out, in the short run it seems likely that the dropped-out veterans will multiply. The movement is at a point of disarray and stalemate: the role of professional radical is less appealing than before; the more recent waves of activists are still less attached to career definitions than the activists of the old New Left, and might therfore find it more natural to drop out.

III

In the minimum future these are roles that do not add up to a movement—a movement requires a shared direction, a strategy for taking power (and then giving it up), a strategy that makes sense of individual contributions. The movement of the sixties is moribund, much of its energies exhausted, its coherence scattered, its novelty gone the way of dogma and fad. Thousands of activists can come together for a show of force against the war, but there is little sustained, out-going activity between the periodic mobilizations. More ominous yet, SDS, the central organizational pivot of the movement in the sixties, left no trace but a wake of sectarian fragments when it disintegrated in 1969—no strategy, no program, and no prospects for mass organization. How to explain the paradox—growing radicalization and shrinking organization, growing disaffection and growing aimlessness? Repression? Real enough, though repression can sometimes organize opposition perforce. Despair, cynicism, weariness at beating one's head against the wall? Yes, all that, but why are these conditions so pervasive and paralytic? Failure to develop a strategy? Also true, but why the failure, when so many radicals enunciated the need? Plenty of self-defeating attitudes, but why are they so common? All these explanations are epiphenomenal. The answer must be sought in the very core of the movement's social identity.

The movement of the sixties arose from a historically unprecedented social base, the emerging stratum of educated labor created by the post-World War II advancement of American capitalism and its need for drastically increased numbers of skilled technical and managerial types. Previous radical student movements had been tiny eruptions of marginal intellectuals, but ours was the first to embody the disaffection of a socially and economically central sector of the population. (More students demonstrated in Washington in May 1971 than existed in all of Russia in the nineteenth century.) Because the base of the movement in the sixties was socially significant, because the movement had a consciousness of its own oppression and, at least implicitly, a sense of its own needs, it could sometimes (student power, street confrontations, youth enclaves) try to stand on its own. In the absence of radical movement elsewhere in the society, it could even claim that it was the embryo of revolutionary agency itself ("we are the people")—a movement *for itself*. In other moments (community and factory organizing), it tried to repudiate its social reality by claiming to be the instrument, or the vanguard, or the catalyst, of social forces that *really* were oppressed (the poor, blacks, industrial workers, the Third World) and capable of taking power— a movement *for others*. Throughout the sixties the movement oscillated between these poles, searching more for identity than for strategy: unable to take the strategic debate seri- ously or to devise post-student organization because it was preoccupied with identity and because in its isolation from the rest of American society it felt compelled to take on every political responsibility at once. As the for-itself mood proved incapable of making change (climaxing in Chicago, August 1968), the movement became uneasy with its vision and the privilege of its social base; as the war accelerated, the pressure on for-itself identity became fiercer; finally, in the name of Marxism, or loyalty to the world proletariat (and specifically to Vietnam), the movement proceeded to drown its novelty and to deny its right to exist for itself. In the process, of course, it became rather useless to others, since it could do little for others unless it were first organized in its own behalf. Unable to carry the burden of historical novelty, sects within SDS (Progressive Labor, Weatherman, Revolu- tionary Youth Movement) took on pseudo-identities as self- appointed vanguards and fifth columns of other forces. Thus they could hold onto their elitist belief in their right to rule, while claiming to have entered the revolutionary lists in the name of their chosen constituencies. They split and devoured SDS so easily because they capitalized on a widespread self- doubt; with a rush they occupied a vacuum of identity and strategy, virtually without opposition. Identity politics swal- lowed itself. The alternative, a conscious, programmatic radicalism, has not yet formed.[4]

---

[4] I have developed this argument in detail in "The Dynamics of the New Left," *Motive 30* (October/November 1970).

Still, there are thousands of activists whose opposition is embedded in some kind of political work, and some loose and heterogeneous sense of "movement" will apply for at least the foreseeable future. But that sense will be sentimental and misleading if political work is simply a personal choice, and "membership" in the movement merely a pledge of allegiance. It is possible for the movement to be political and antipolitical at the same time—to express needs that can only be met through political change, while having no idea how that change is to come about or how to move the country toward it. This is roughly the current state of things. Embroiled in episodic events, empty polemic, terrorism, and, at best, as in the women's movement and some youth enclaves, attempts to secure a sense of political identity and community, most movement activists fail to estimate the political *effect* of their work, to understand it in the context of capitalist development, and to visualize a clear trajectory forward. Strategy depends on a grasp of the forces at work in the society, yet the politics of the real world—the flux of high-level decisions, national parties, bureaucracies—has so discredited itself over the last ten years that it often seems hardly worthwhile to pay attention to the dry maneuvers, the hollow rhetoric, the parliamentary shuffles, the predictable defaults, and the names behind the guns. But ugly and foreign as they are to the movement sensibility, these shifts and intimations bear watching.

The activists' achievement over a decade, along with that of the black movement, has been to make visible, and sometimes to mobilize, the opposition that is helplessly manufactured by the failure of the social system itself; to break the hold of bourgeois ideology and to make radical ideas legitimate; and to intimate political alternatives. The movement as a crystallization of social instability has also become a social problem in itself, a scapegoat for widespread social dissatisfaction and the target of reactionary consolidation. But there has been another effect, the joint product of the movement's insurgency and the social system's failure. Long overdue, and perhaps too late, liberal forces have begun, barely begun, to appreciate the magnitude of the social crisis and to gather the desire, if not the will or the momentum, for reform. The Democrats' attempt in Congress to wrest control of the war from the Nixon Administration is a sign of a revival of life in the political system; so is their rejection of the SST and of Haynsworth and Carswell. The momentum of the McGovern campaign; *the Wall Street Journal's* recognition that the war is playing havoc with the balance of payments; John Gardner's organization of Common Cause—a liberal middle-class lobby; the stand of several churches against the war; the spread of antimilitary feeling in liberal circles; the CBS broadcast of *The Selling of the Pentagon*; and *Life* Magazine's attack on J. Edgar Hoover; the talk about the need for "new priorities," an end to the arms race, domestic reconstruction—all are traces of a leftward motion from the center. In another light, they are intimations of a split in the ruling class between garrison-state hard-liners and corporate liberals. One striking feature of this ferment is that the emerging liberal program is a watered-down version of the reform program recommended by SDS in 1962: an East-West detente, paceful accommodation with Third World liberation movements, disarmament, a completion of the welfare state, income redistribution, full employment, an end to race discrimination, and so forth. SDS thought then that existing liberal forces, prompted by a small, but perceptive and dogged left, could absorb this program. As it turned out, liberalism's halting modernization has required the assertion of the left itself as a social force. *But the fact that liberalism has taken so long simply to begin to assume its logical program indicates how flabby it has been,* how compromised its politics, and how weak and corrupt its organization.

Blind faith in the triumph of liberalism is clearly misplaced; however logical as the *sine qua non* of social stability, liberalism is still the consciousness of a minority in the power centers. The new stirrings amount to a mood more than a program. Indeed liberalism has already failed, fuel in the furnace of the Indochina war. War on poverty, black capitalism, and liberal mayors have all failed or gone down to defeat. The most revealing sign of liberalism's impotence is the fact that the war continues. However rational it seems to end the war— even from an imperialist viewpoint, considering the military drain and demoralization, the economic and political costs, not to mention the murder—the fact is that four successive administrations have found other motives more compelling.

However, all in all, a liberal return to power seems more likely than not, if only by default. Without unduly crediting the rationality of the ruling class, we can say that liberal power centers will have two strong incentives to pull their forces together. First, negatively, their fear of populist reaction if the country continues to slide into chaos and breakdown; and second, positively, the promise of a victorious electoral coalition composed of blue-collar workers and minorities, who want economic and racial reforms, and the growing numbers of youth and others, who want retrenchment in foreign policy and progress in ecology. This could be the electoral base that dominates the seventies and eighties. The lessening salience of the "social issue"—campus unrest, "crime in the streets," "moral decay"—according to recent polls, is some evidence that the white ethnic constituencies and middle classes will probably not be satisfied with scapegoating in a time of inflation, growing unemployment, and war: but if the Democratic party is to hold these groups, it must offer concrete reforms. So there is some reason to think that by 1976, if not 1972, reformers will be in power—if it is not hallucinatory to think that far ahead, past the possibilities of world war and nuclear nightmare.

Whether and how long liberal reforms could actually reduce discontent is something else again. Substantial federal aid, made possible by military cutbacks (with or without progressive tax reform that Muskie would shy away from), could perhaps arrest the deterioration of the cities and pacify the blacks for a while—a decade or two. Keynesian measures could avert or postpone economic crisis. Kennedy-style national health insurance and other federal financing of services (even guaranteed income) could forestall radical alternatives and alleviate some of the worst impoverishment. The preeminent question is whether such a liberal administration would dare to end the war. If it does, withdrawal of all troops and airpower from Southeast Asia, coupled with continuing revolt in the Army, could make the next intervention much more difficult; a radical movement could take credit for an enormous victory. If it doesn't, if bombing continues under the cover of Vietnamization and the administration persists in support of Thieu, the antiwar movement would be unlikely to be placated any more than it has been by Nixon.

In any event, since liberalism is not likely to mount an assault on corporate prerogatives, the fiscal crisis of the state—the pauperization of the state as it is compelled to provide more and more services to compensate for the fail-

ures and usurpations of the corporate economy—would continue; the tax burden would continue to fall on the lower
strata; and imperialism, more rational, less military, would
persist. Liberalism would probably not even substantially
lighten the load of repression, as liberals to date have been
unable or unwilling to curb growing police power and localized
fascism. A liberal regime would be neither just nor radical,
but if it ends the war it could give radicals some badly needed
time and psychic space in which to breathe, resolve internal
tensions, creep out from under the paralyzing threat of apoc-
alypse, formulate programs, and build an organization. Of
course it would finally betray hopes, but a radical movement
would have little to fear from that.

Paradoxically, liberalism could occupy the heights of the
society as radicalism continues to swarm at the bottom.
For liberalism would not touch the deepest sources of discontent: managerial usurpation of power in work place,
school, and family. Reforms are very unlikely to sweep so
far as to eliminate the oppressiveness of institutions, whether
factories over workers or universities over students, for the
proletarianization of the population is inherent in the dynamic
of capitalism. Some activists might be defused by an end to
the war, but is this to say that the left needs the war? In
fact at the same time that the war illuminates the need for
revolutionary change, it is as profoundly destructive to the left
as to the rest of the country: it heightens desperation and
diverts, *necessarily diverts,* attention from the needs of the
American segment of a global revolution. In the interest
of remaining life in Indochina, no apology should be necessary
for the need to end the war—by whatever means necessary.
If liberals can be forced to do the job that the left has tried
its damnedest to do for six years, then some power to the
liberals.

To summarize: in the minimum future, radicals will have
sounded the alarm and liberals will have answered it. The
activists will have taken political initiative only to have lost
it again (because of isolation of class and consciousness) to
forces that are actually organized to govern. The activists will
march through institutions and inhabit communes as individuals, clusters, and small scattered functional groups, not as a
concerted movement with magnetic force for the majority
outside the political counter-culture. Radical work will con-

tinue in youth enclaves, universities, professions, and here and there in factories, offices, and schools, but the political whole will be no greater than the sum of its parts.

IV

The maximum future subsumes the minimum—the elaboration of full-time activist roles, radical professional roles as well as dropout explorations, and the likelihood of liberal resurgence. What could convert the minimum into the maximum would be the development of an organized, radical cross-class movement, which seems conceivable, if not certainly foreordained, by 1984.

The structural features of an organized movement are easier to visualize than the social prerequisites. The movement would federate local, broad-based insurgent groups, engaged in struggles to achieve power in communities, cities, and a few states, with functional groups, active within work places and specific institutions. Among the functions of such a federation would be:

1. To devise a decentralized socialist program that expresses a common understanding of the needs of the American population without masking the necessary tensions among federated groups; a program that insists on the principle of workers' control and on the need to contest corporate power over war, environment, resources, health, etc.; a program that is both practical and visionary.
2. To coordinate political work among those already in motion.
3. To help disparate and sometimes opposed insurgent groups discover a common interest.
4. To choose priorities for new organizing ventures, so that a student or dangling radical may know where he is needed.
5. To train catalytic organizers.
6. To develop fruitful debates over theory. To provide media for reports on the testing of theory by practice, as well as media to convey the program to unorganized people.
7. To experiment with modes of leadership that minimize elitism.

What I have in mind is obviously not a Leninist party, not a shadow government, but a well-articulated network of relationships among local and functional groups which works to bolster those groups and would take on only certain well-defined and limited, though important, tasks in addition. It would not itself prepare to take power, but rather reach and activate a mass movement, and develop an infrastructure of organization ("a new society within the shell of the old") for which the possibility of power would be imaginable. It would not be afraid to fight for reforms—what André Gorz has called "non-reformist reforms"—the campaigns for which would illuminate the necessity and possibility of democratic power, and which, if achieved, would enlarge the scope of bottom-up power and whet the appetite for more.

Such a provisional radical "organization"—though it would not be as rigid as that word has come to imply—is possible only if some critical mass of local and functional groups exists first, because only roots in such groups would give it legitimacy as more than the creature of a handful of intellectuals, say, or of a particular sect. So far there exists only a handful of constituent groups, mainly black workers' caucuses, professional networks, and youth enclave associations.

This fact points to the central obstacle preventing a gathering of radical forces: the class isolation of the existing white movement. The activists of the sixties and early seventies, again, come primarily from the upper social layers, and have proved largely incapable of spreading *actionable* radical consciousness to industrial workers, the white poor, secretaries, tellers, clerks, housewives, computer programmers, teachers, . . . police. (The single important exception is the GI movement, which has benefited from ex-student organizers, at least up to a point.) Almost every movement project that promised systematic outreach—Mississippi Summer, SDS's community organizing projects, Vietnam Summer, work-ins, People's Peace Treaty, etc.—foundered on the rock of the organizers' programless insularity. Driven by a combination of moral fervor and guilt, unable to satisfactorily explain their presence in foreign cultures, organizers responded to suspicion and inertia ("apathy") by lapsing into elitist behavior, which in turn heightened the "apathy" of the unorganized. It is not so much that the organizers did not know what to propose, but that they did not know much about their constituency's culture and needs, did not know how to listen, observe, and translate observation into program and tactic.

But the imposing fact is that organization by outsiders who are not exquisitely careful is almost inescapably elitist and probably, even in its own terms, ineffective *if the constituency has not begun to mobilize itself.* For this reason, cross-class national organization awaits the self-mobilization of the unorganized—coherent organization arising from rank-and-file trade-union revolts (especially over control of the work process), white-collar and lower-professional insurgencies, deep-rooted community organizations, especially in the ghettos. There are beginnings in all of these areas, especially among black workers, but they are only beginnings. As these stirrings are heard, the ex-student activists may help—with a variety of specific skills as well as political programs which clearly show the interdependence of one sector's needs with another's. Without the self-mobilization of workers, the plant-gate leaflet that "explains the worker's immediate grievances in a larger perspective" is just another piece of paper. The much touted "worker-student alliance" awaits the revolt of the workers, which student and ex-student activists can herald but not really hasten. To be sure, movement antiauthoritarianism and radical politics have proved somewhat infectious among the lower-class young, penetrating junior colleges, high schools, and the Army, which among them will graduate many of the next generations of young workers—but the movement has not done much directly to help fix antiauthoritarian attitudes into clear political understanding and program. Should these attitudes crystallize on the job, the working classes and the ex-student activists might end up that much closer together. But even in this eventuality there would remain enormous difficulties in achieving a common program that would take account of the young activists' post-scarcity vision without merely consolidating their class privilege vis-à-vis the lower classes. And that racial and sexual suspicions would over-shadow even those of class goes without saying. Relations between the socialist federation and black and feminist movements would have to be worked out with a sensitivity born of great finesse as well as need.

And even other obstacles loom before the prospect of an organized radical movement. The aging ex-student activists have a long way to go to overcome the comfortable and (to the perpetrators) rewarding habits of elitism and male chauvinism. Self-admonition and *mea culpa* have become routine—and largely empty. What is required is more than observation of the crimes; but an understanding of their deep roots in our socialized psyches: finally, each activist must become aware of his *own* victimization by the social system and make that the primary ground of his political being. Aware of his own stake in revolutionary change, and his own socially-bred limitations, he is less likely to trample on the rights of The Others he stoops, altruistically, to organize. But so much of the movement's arrogance is embedded in the reality of its social origins, the institutions of its nurturance, and most poignantly in the need to do something for Vietnam: that arrogance will not be easy to uproot.

Nor will the impatience, implanted by childhoods of imme-diate gratification and nurtured by television's propensity for instant solutions, and finally heightened by the sense of ur-gency to end the war, which leads activists to seek quick-frozen Marxist-Leninist ideology and apocalyptic symbolic violence, and ends in demoralization, crack-up, and terrorism when change is not forthcoming. Nor the activists' contempt for the Americans locked into their consumptive traps. Nor the attitude that a revolution is property, the exclusive posses-sion of the faction with the reddest book or the most extrava-gant rhetoric. Nor the substitution of chants for concrete analysis, or sentiment for theory, guns and self-sacrifice for strategy, or "vanguard" for mass.

V

Optimists call this moment a transitional period. Many young activists are confused and deeply troubled, trying to take stock of failures and deep dilemmas built into the history of the past decade, trying to find strength to keep working under severe pressure without clear guidelines. Does the movement exist? The intuitive answer shifts from day to day. The move-ment is everywhere and nowhere; it exists perhaps as a disembodied Idea, a historical ghost come too early or too late; and as Tom Nairn has pointed out, sectarianism emerges as the combat for possession of a revolution that is only an Idea. If the movement exists it exists despite itself, because so many people need to believe in it—a curious and fragile form of existence indeed.

In any case, the *organized* radical movement of the sixties

is wrecked and obsolete, a victim of its own spirited innocence, its driven quest for identity substituting for conscious
politics, its acceptance of too heavy a historical burden. Not
only was the movement's social base—educated labor—a new
phenomenon in history, occasioning a feeling of surprise and
confusion that the movement should exist at all, but the movement was in many ways marginal to potential power and
desperate to compensate for marginality with political hubris.
It had all the pathologies of intellectuals and, because of its
ambitions, few of the advantages.

But also a large part of the trouble was that, in a sense, the
movement was forced to give birth to itself. Throughout the
sixties, the Marxist-Leninist remnants offered analyses of
imperialism, but were largely discredited by Stalinism; the
social democrats offered a verbal insistence on democracy,
until the Mississippi blacks pleaded for it in 1964; the honor-
able pacifists offered at least an insistence on direct action;
but none of them offered any clear understanding of the structure and texture and flow of contemporary American society,
and none of them stood for a live movement; and so the movement was forced to patch together a world view with scraps
of leftover theory and intuition, sewed together with moralism
and with faith in youth and our own experience. Youth was
overvalued because there were few elders to emulate, and
moralism had to serve as a substitute for ideas that were left
unrepresented by credible advocates. This fragile patchwork
was left virtually alone to combat the most powerful and
arrogant empire in the history of the world. No wonder the
seams could not hold. It seems remarkable that the movement survived as long as it did, spread as many waves, met
as many responsibilities, engendered as much fresh analysis,
expressed as much energy.

The movement choked on its own myths, but myths like
cowards die many times and still clutch life. Some radicals
heralded the counter-culture as a here-and-now embodiment
of liberation; but the myth of the Age of Aquarius went down
in anomie and blood at Altamont, in the bodies of Jimi
Hendrix and Janis Joplin, in syringes of smack and speed, in
John Lennon's "The Dream Is Over." Some held to the myth
of the movement itself as the new society aborning; that myth
died again and again and finally in the SDS debacle. Some
believed in salvation by following the most oppressed and,

therefore, presumably more clear-sighted blacks; that myth fell with the fratricide in the Black Panther party. And some believed that the revolutionary climax was imminent, a kind of projection of the internal clock that has been stuck for years at a minute to midnight; that myth died in a Greenwich Village townhouse. Each myth displaced clarity and each persists. Yet a movement of the seventies and eighties could begin with considerable advantages. There are ten years of proximate experience to be explored, codified, and made generally accessible. There is something of a new political culture that offers some—not nearly enough—practical models of radical work and some protection. There is some awareness of the evils of male dominance, self-righteousness, encapsulation ("Berkeley is America"). And with the patent failure of the political system and the decay of prevailing ideology, radical ideas are coming to have a legitimacy in many layers of the society, which could encourage imagination and energy.

There are scattered signs of new possibilities. If there is much despair and self-delusion among radicals, there is also something of a new realism bubbling beneath the public surface of self-celebratory underground media and extravagant rhetoric. There is not only a modest upwelling of analysis and self-criticism on the left, mostly in *Liberation* magazine and in privately circulated papers, but more important, the unavoidable insistence of the women's movement that a revolutionary movement cannot be allowed to replicate the pathologies of the larger society. Yet finally myths persist past their time when they are not supplanted by more plausible ideas. At the moment, there is no sign of strategy or actionable political program generally agreed upon. The new awareness inhabits a political vacuum.

The question is not whether there will be a revolution by 1984 but whether there will be a credible mass revolutionary *movement,* strategically located in production, bent on democracy, capable of taking and remaking power. If an unprecedented revolution is not just felt to be necessary for The Others, but for oneself; if it is understood as a process in which a revolutionary integrates his life, love, and work, without contempt for others who do not; then the powerful and joyful and sustaining sense of a movement's We may reemerge— this time not as an exclusive identity, defined by moral superiority to The Others; not as a Judeo-Christian gift to The

Others; but as an I-Thou confluence that defines itself more by inclusion than by exclusion, that makes it natural if not easy for The Others to feel themselves and to be a part of the process of conscious change. A new movement could perform the long-overdue and historically appropriate marriage between socialism and anarchism, expressing a practical vision of decentralized power that banishes once and for all the powerful ghost of Stalin. It could span an age continuum which gives the young models of useful roles to grow into. Such a movement could make "revolution" more than a rallying cry or a statement of urgent and inchoate needs, but a plausible image of the future anchored in concrete programs and the feeling-tone and organization of the movement itself. Or by 1984 the We might have disintegrated, partly absorbed and partly repressed, into a vague allegiance barely concealing a congeries of mutually suspicious and politically marginal clusters, sealed in obsolete ideology, making some concrete changes but unable to use victories to achieve momentum for more, hopping from project to project without truly absorbing the lessons of any, pugnacious, anomic, more acted upon than acting—swimming in the sea of radical consciousness, but not swimming anywhere in particular.

There is plenty of historical precedent for both futures, and both tendencies are alive. Which is to prevail depends in part on the opening of the political system, the possibility of real changes that a movement causes and then transcends, the pace and extensiveness of radicalization throughout the society, and on political-economic factors so chancy that speculation seems pointless. But more pointedly, the future of the young activists hangs, as always on choices, on irreducible will. Can the volcanic women's movement face inward ("consciousness-raising") and outward (program and organizing, especially among working women) at the same time? Will there be a new and wiser wave of radical student organization? Will the youth enclaves become bases for forays into the rest of America, rather than enclosed voluntary reservations, internal exile colonies, for freaks, radicals, and utopian experimenters? Will radicalism in the work place and community come to overshadow the radicalism that thrives parasitically on capitalist fat? Will radical professionals maintain momentum? No one knows. But even today's young radicals would have great political weight if they could reconcile leadership with democracy and organization with initiative from the bottom, if they could get out from under media definitions of radicalism, if they could take seriously the need for new theory and vision . . . one tires of ifs. Despite the present stalemate, more than any other American left of the last fifty years the young activists have a chance to free themselves of mystification and to be "new" not just chronologically but in ideology, style, and consequence. So much of the chance for change and hope and a decent life hangs in the balance that it seems absurd to count the consequences.

GENE L. MASON

a political scientist at Franconia College, was arrested during the early stages of a mounting Congressional campaign in the sixth district in Kentucky. At the time of this publication, he is serving a one-year sentence at the Kentucky State Penitentiary at La Grange. His direct experiences with repression in the case are described in *The Politics of Exploitation* (Random House, 1973), which he coedited.

---

the future
of repression

In modern industrial society man has inherited manifold controls over his behavior. The one form of control with which we are all familiar is bureaucratic. Anyone who tells of his frustrations with organizations that order human activity—bureaucratic control groups—strikes a responsive cord in his audience. Individual defeat is a common experience, whether the organization is a so-called public utility, the Internal Revenue Service, the Social Security Administration, a school, or any number of complex organizations. These are not isolated phenomena: as society becomes more densely populated and more technologically sophisticated, controls increase.

Despite the fact that much of our condition is inherited, we must ask ourselves, as indeed every generation must, how much control we are willing to tolerate. When the level of control is greater than desired, we call it repression. Repression is a condition of deprivation in the development of freedom, resulting from the imposition of controls through ordering human activity. The classic depiction of total repression is in George Orwell's *1984,* in which all are slaves—the proles, the outer and the inner party members. He projected a totalitarian repression more sophisticated and more complete than ever before envisaged. The citizens of *1984* not only experience external repression of their conscious behavior—terror, highly efficient surveillance, coercion, and control of movement—but also incredibly complex external control of their unconscious mental processes—thought control it is called. There are thought crimes that can be avoided only by so internalizing the standards of the regime that thought deviation is not likely to be a possibility. They unconsciously acquiesce in totalitarianism. Writing in 1948, Orwell dated the projections 1984, now only a decade away.

Our 1984 will not be his. Repression will not be complete; but it will be greater than we have ever experienced. Unlike *1984*, repression has never been evenly distributed in our society. The roots of repression are the basic differences among us: social and economic class, race, sex, life style, political orientation, and age. These differences enhance the disposition to repress experienced by people in positions of power. The economically and politically powerless experience

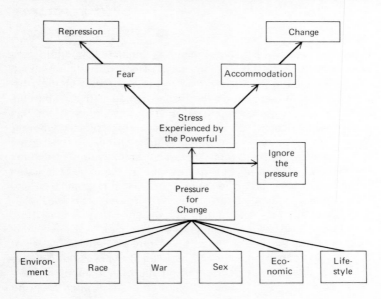

the most repression; and the most powerful, the least. But the level of repression is related not only to the distribution of differences (power, for example), but to the total amount of stress the society is experiencing. A social and political system undergoes great stress when political orientations are polarized and extensive demands for substantial change are placed on it. Figure 1 may help clarify the relationship between the issues of social change stemming from our differences and the possible responses of the powerful agents of control. Note that the powerful can respond to pressure for change by ignoring it (President Nixon watching a football game when thousands of antiwar demonstrators protested outside the White House) or, once that pressure reaches a certain level of intensity, either meeting the demands for change or repressing those who demand it.[1] Naturally, people of power may do some of both, and, as we shall see, frequently do.

I

The history of repression in twentieth-century America will give nightmares to the untutored. Every period of economic instability and every war have produced domestic repression. World War I, World War II, Korea—all have been preceded and followed by periods of economic instability. (Today we are experiencing these phenomena of war, economic instability, and repression simultaneously.) Pacifists, anarchists, and other radicals protesting United States participation in World War I were deftly hidden from view in jails across the country or summarily deported. During the "Red Scare" of the 1920s Attorney General Palmer jailed, in one night, thousands of people he considered dangerous. Christian pacifists who carried their religious precepts into the secular world were imprisoned throughout World War II.[2] Men who had labor deferments and who went on strike were threatened with induction. More than 112,000 Japanese Americans were evacuated in 1942 and imprisoned in concentration camps, an

[1] Another possible response in the face of stress is psychological withdrawal.

[2] Some of their prison experiences are described in a fantastic but rare movement document. See Holley Cantine and Dachine Rainer (eds.), *Prison Etiquette* (Bearsville, N.Y.: Retort Press, 1950).

event without precedent in American history.[3] We are hard-pressed to scorn the atrocities of Hitler or other modern dictators when parts of our own history could easily have been episodes from a totalitarian handbook.

After World War II the U.S. Supreme Court became more concerned with enforcing toleration of our differences and protecting individual rights. But the thrust of all our institutions is not always in the same direction. The Smith Act, passed by Congress in 1940, was used to imprison members of the Socialist Workers party in 1941. The same act was used in 1948 to destroy the top leadership of the Communist party. They spent five years in prison for "conspiring" to "advocate" violent overthrow of the government. Get that— "conspiring" to "advocate"! They were rearrested as soon as they were released in 1954. When they were in prison, 119 additional Communist party officials were arrested or indicted on "conspiracy." The McCarran-Walter Act, passed during an intensely emotional period in 1952, allowed the federal government to "arrest without warrant, detain for an indefinite period, and conduct hearings without due process against aliens."[4] During the early 1950s Senator Joseph McCarthy of Wisconsin, and those who supported him, used the communism issue to create national hysteria. "The Politics of Fear," as one writer described it,[5] affected tens of thousands of Americans by jail sentences, by occupational blacklisting and by inculcating a fear of massive subversion in their own government.

We have never been without local episodes of repression—sporadic for most, but systematic for many. Slavery, then thousands of lynchings, and always total—or is it totalitarian—repression for blacks. This is at the heart of our history. Repression and official lawlessness in the South were made

---

[3] Morton Grodzins, *Americans Betrayed: Politics and the Japanese Evacuation* (Chicago: University of Chicago Press, 1949), p. 362. All of these examples are modern versions of the ancient but misguided premise that if you hide something from view or avoid looking at it, it will go away, known in some quarters as the Toilet Assumption.

[4] Mike Honey, "Back to the '50's: The Latest in Repressive Legislation," *Motive* 30 (December 1970), p. 53.

[5] Robert Griffith, *The Politics of Fear* (Lexington: University of Kentucky Press, 1970).

visible in the early 1960s.[6] (As a nation we waited until the 1968 Democratic Convention in Chicago to see it work in the North.) It took demonstrations, confrontations, and deaths to highlight the injustice perpetrated on blacks. Those who participated learned something of repression. Those who did not already know it learned that when one group is systematically oppressed by the established economic, social, and political systems, attempts to alter the inhumanity of this system result in the forces of authority being waged. Control techniques, as law enforcement officials are apt to call instruments of repression, are brought to bear. And the cycle of oppression, reaction, fear, repression starts all over again. Everyday life for the oppressed becomes fraught with fearful expectations; and were it not in America, it would be called terror.

II

The magnified visibility of external repression has not led to its reduction. If anything, it appears to be expanding in two ways: proportionately more people are experiencing intolerable control of their behavior by the state, and the techniques of repression—controls and sanctions that agents of power impose—are more severe. While the existence of some repression is probably obvious to us all, its expansion is not. This is no accident. As Barrington Moore reminds us, it is easy today to confuse objectivity with conventional judiciousness and with triviality and meaninglessness:

> Any simple straight forward truth about political institutions or events is bound to have polemical consequences. It will damage some group interest. In any society the dominant groups are the ones with the most to hide about the way the society works. Very often therefore truthful analyses are bound to have a critical ring, to seem like exposures rather than objective statements, as the term is conventionally used. . . . For all students of human society sympathy for the victims of historical processes and skepticism about the victors' claims provide essential safeguards against being taken in by the dominant mythology.[7]

[6] A very careful and creative examination of the factors that restrict the visibility of evil is Lewis Coser, "The Visibility of Evil," *Journal of Social Issues,* 25, 1 (1969), 100–109.

[7] Barrington Moore, *Social Origins of Dictatorship and Democracy* (Boston: Beacon Press, 1969), pp. 522–523.

When repression is increasing, we expect authorities to insist rigidly that nothing unusual is going on.[8]

But repression is increasing with support from substantial segments of the public. If we use mail coming into the offices of Chiefs of Police across the country as the measure, public support for police attacks on others during the urban civil disorders of the second half of the 1960s ran in excess of 99 percent.[9] The pattern was the same whether we look at Watts, Detroit, Newark, or the series of riots following the assassination of Martin Luther King. Even the highly visible behavior of police in Chicago during the 1968 Democratic Convention, when the objects of police overkill were white middle-class young people, not blacks, resulted in two-thirds of the American public expressing their support.[10] More recently a Louis Harris poll found the public opposed to even peaceful demonstrations by students by a margin of 52 to 38 percent.[11] The Bill of Rights could never stand the test of a public referendum. Majority sentiment is highly supportive of repression, and those in power act accordingly.

In our society, politically polarized and plagued by fear, there is no successful way of avoiding this dilemma: either we will attempt to deal with the causes of disorders or we will increase repression. No less than five presidential commissions have studied this situation intensely, and all have called for immediate efforts toward long-term social justice. This is the central message of the Katzenbach (Crime), Kerner (Civil Disorders), Eisenhower (Violence), Walker (Chicago Convention), and Scranton (Campus Violence) reports. The last four of these reports specifically warn against increasing repression. With the exception of the Crime Commission, whose recommendations have been implemented in large numbers, each successive presidential administration seems content to place these reports on the shelves and to reserve their recommendations for further study and prayer. When they aren't ignored, they are cursed outright: Vice President Spiro Agnew denounced the Scranton report as "pablum for

---

[8] See Charles Reich's comments on this point in *Law and Social Action* (Winter 1970), p. 10.

[9] Ramsey Clark, *Crime in America* (New York: Pocket, 1971), p. 148.

[10] Richard Harris, *Justice* (New York: Dutton, 1970), p. 69.

[11] *Ibid.,* p. 186.

permissivists." Instead of attacking the causes of the malaise, we find more national support for the stockpiling of weapons by local police and the passage of new, more repressive legislation.

The recent Law Enforcement Assistance Act, incorporating recommendations of the Crime Commission, has facilitated such stockpiling. It grants money to the states and gives them the option of determining how their grants are to be spent. The stockpiling of the latest weaponry has been one result.[12] The act has enormous potential for turning disorder into massacre, because, very simply, it augments the brute force with which the state can respond to a domestic crisis. New businesses have sprung up all over the country simply to act as the purchasing agents for local police in their desire to increase their arsenal. After all, that is what Congress gave them the money for.

If one doubts that such an arsenal will ever be used by the police to repress a disturbance, he need only look closely at recent history. When state troopers and national guardsmen seized Attica State Prison in September 1971, they relied on heavy caliber shotgun ammunition that sprayed imprecisely through the prison yard crowded with inmates and guards taken as hostages. The inmates had expected tear gas and rubber bullets; instead, each shell contained ten 32-caliber slugs that spread out in a widening pattern. The bodies of seven hostages and four inmates were pelleted with this ammunition. The use of overkill in urban riots is a familiar pattern. The college campus is no more immune:

Berkeley Park (May 15, 1969). On the campus of the University of California a "People's Park" was erected on a vacant lot owned by the university. The Board of Regents had other plans

---

[12] One weapon frequently purchased is the AR-15 automatic rifle. In a slightly modified from (5.56 mm rifle M16A1), it is currently issued to most Army units in Vietnam. It can fire 700–900 rounds a minute and has a muzzle velocity of 3250 feet-per-second, accurate at 460 meters. Its reverberations are so severe that a person hit by it in the foot will likely die from shock. It was designed for killing human beings. I discovered a number of these weapons being carried by Lexington, Kentucky policemen on the campus of the University of Kentucky during a campus confrontation after the Cambodian invasion in 1970. When I asked Assistant Police Chief Hedger what possible use there would be for such overkill, he said they might be necessary to knock down a tree or a brick wall to get a sniper.

for the space. The result: the Berkeley police, the California Highway Patrol, and the Alameda County Sheriff's Department moved in to move others out; 110 demonstrators were shot; 13 required hospitalization due to shotgun wounds; 1 died from ⅓-inch buckshot that ripped open his belly at 30 feet; 1 was blinded from being blasted in the face with birdshot. Finally the National Guard cleared the area with tear gas sprayed from a helicopter. During that week, 1,000 were arrested and 200 booked on felony charges.

Orangeburg (March 1968). Black students at South Carolina State College demonstrated for three days against a segregated bowling alley near the campus. Local police, state troopers, and a National Guard company were sent in to control students at the virtually all-black campus. Total police presence out-numbered the students. Without warning police opened fire at point-blank range, killing 3 and wounding 27 others. Of those killed, 1 had been shot five times in the back and side, and 1 had been shot six times in the back and side and once above the heart. Most of the students injured were shot while lying on the ground. They were hit in the back and in the bottom of the feet. One policeman emptied his revolver at the crowd.

Kent State (May 4, 1970). Shortly after noon, a beautiful shiny day, students at KSU were demonstrating against U.S. expansion of the Vietnam war into Cambodia. National Guardsmen were summoned by Governor Rhodes directly from riot duty in the Cleveland area, where, on April 29, a wildcat Teamsters' strike had violently erupted. Many teamsters and guardsmen were injured. Rhodes fixed an 8:00 PM curfew, but the ROTC building was burned down two hours later. The guardsmen moved onto the campus, and in one of the resulting confrontations 4 students were shot to death, and 9 others were injured, 3 seriously. The FBI report said buckshot, rifle slugs, a sub-machine gun, and carbines with armor piercing bullets were used in the fusillade against the students. The FBI found the marks of nearly 400 bullets on Alexander Hall alone, but the shell casings and empty cartridges disappeared.[13]

The power of police is more immense today than ever before in American history. There are more laws for them to enforce,

[13] This list is limited out of considerations of space. The evidence should also include Jackson State in Mississippi and other campuses where the experiences are similar. The interested reader should consult the Scranton Report on Campus Violence.

and their ability to do so, especially in curbing civil disorders, is greater. And when the police themselves break the law, as they have been prone to do in these situations, police power is even more dangerous. If police are lawless, there is no one to enforce the law. Increased repression is not only likely, it is inevitable. A lawless police state is the result.

One lesson of our recent history is that if police break the law to accomplish the tasks they set for themselves and their public expects of them, the law will soon be changed to legitimize their actions. If the behavior of those they engage is not criminal, new laws will be passed to criminalize their actions. Our country is already highly criminalized: we define more acts as illegal, and the sanctions for them tend to be more severe than in any advanced industrial society in the western world.[14] At a recent conference on "Crime and Punishment" sponsored by the Center for the Study of Democratic Institutions, attended by a wide range of law enforcement officials and academics, including a representative of [then] Attorney General Mitchell's Justice Department, there was widespread agreement that our society must be "decriminalized."[15] Norval Morris of the University of Chicago Law School, in describing the overreach of our criminal laws to such things as drunkenness, drugs, gambling, disorderly conduct, vagrancy, abortion, sexual behavior, and juvenile delinquency, said, "I think that of roughly six and a half million arrests per year in America, three million are a complete waste of time."[16] Decriminalization would undercut the arguments advanced in favor of a wide range of repressive laws. Many social problems we criminalize could and should be dealt with in other ways.

Official government response has been more criminalization, not less. After the urban riots had run their course and the disturbances on college campuses were capturing the attention of everyone, legislation was being churned out of Wash-

[14] Bruce Jackson, "Our Prisons are Criminal," *The New York Times Magazine,* September 28, 1968.

[15] Decriminalization means striking from the books all offenses that do not damage the person or property of others, where there is no victim and no complainant.

[16] Norval Morris, cited in "Crime and Punishment in America," *The Center Magazine* 4 (May/June 1971), p. 12.

ington and the state capitals to "deal" with these new enemies of the republic. In the spring of 1968, Congress passed the now famous conspiracy-to-riot statute, the Rap Brown law. The 1968 law defined a riot as "an act or acts of violence" by anyone in an "assemblage of three or more persons" that endangered or damaged any person or any property. Three persons! The effect of the law was to discourage demonstrations and to provide another basis for prosecuting dissidents. Any person who crossed a state line to participate in a demonstration and got involved in a fight with at least three people— even if started by policemen—could be arrested. If convicted, he faced five years in prison and a $10,000 fine. It was under this statute that the members of the Chicago Conspiracy were tried in Judge Hoffman's court. More recently the Seattle Conspiracy faced similar charges.[17]

The Seattle case demonstrates how the government has used *agents provocateurs* to assist and encourage people to break the law. This case involved a demonstration protesting the verdict of the Chicago Seven case at the federal court house in Tacoma, Washington. Some windows were broken. Peace symbols were sprayed on the building with spray paint. Months later, seven participants were charged with crossing a state line with the intent to conspire to riot. The FBI informer and *agent provocateur* in this case is a thirty-four-year-old businessman from Seattle who volunteered to join a commune there. He was paid $500 a month, plus all expenses. At the trial he testified to the following:

1. He purchased five pounds of potassium chlorate, a chemical used to ignite Molotov cocktails. After the FBI had checked the chemical for purity, he turned it over to others in the group he infiltrated.
2. He offered to provide the group with two cases of dynamite.
3. He provided the leaders of the group with a tear gas gun. He gave instructions to the group on the handling of fire arms, including sniper tactics.
4. He purchased on his FBI expense account a case of spray paint that he knew would be used to spray buildings.

[17] Michael Lerner, who wrote "The Future of the Two-Party System in America" for this volume, was a defendant in the case.

5. The FBI financed his $20 contribution toward the printing of bumper stickers in Seattle which read, "Serve the People. Stop the Pigs!"
6. During his undercover work, he used drugs extensively and purchased on his FBI expense account and distributed to radicals he met large quantities of drugs, including LSD, marijuana, speed, methadrine, and cocaine.
7. He broke the terms of his state-imposed probation (staying off college campuses) on instructions from the FBI, gave up a monogamous relationship with his wife in order to maintain his cover, and agreed to use a militant line in recruiting for the Weathermen.

Not only is the government attempting to control "unorthodox" political activities, it is also attempting to promote them so it can have activities to control. The conspiracy-to-riot statute and the *agent provocateur* are useful tools in a repressive arsenal.

Additional criminalization and repression are found in four comprehensive pieces of crime control legislation. The new measures are:

The Omnibus Crime Control and Safe Streets Act (1968).

The District of Columbia Court Reform and Criminal Procedures Act (1970).

The Organized Crime Control Act (1970).

The Comprehensive Drug Abuse Prevention and Control Act (1970).

Despite substantial clamor over dangerously repressive provisions in each of these acts, they passed by huge majorities in both houses: the Senate voted 73 to 1 for the Organized Crime Control Act and unanimously for the Drug Act. The repressive portions of this package deserve careful scrutiny, more than space allows in this essay. The D.C. Court Reform Act, which the Nixon administration expects to be used as the model for legislation by cities and states, requires that a citizen suing a policeman for false arrest pay for the officer's lawyer even if the citizen wins. Naturally, this promotes arbitrary arrests. It was this provision that facilitated the mass arrests of 12,000 people during the 1971 May Day demonstration.[18]

The Organized Crime Control Act denies defendants access to illegally obtained wiretap evidence and provides for the use of such evidence after five years have elapsed from the time it was obtained.

The provisions that drew the most criticism and that immensely enhance police state powers relate to no-knock, self-incrimination and immunity, extensive wiretapping and bugging, preventive detention, and dangerous special offenders. No-knock is part of the D.C. Court Reform Act and is now applied nationally through the Drug Abuse Prevention and Control Act. It authorizes police to break into and enter homes, buildings, and cars for searching without giving notice of their identity and purpose.[19] The first use of no-knock, outside of the District of Columbia, was in Phoenix, Arizona. The Phoenix police planned a no-knock raid on a couple, described by the police as hippies, who used and pushed drugs. Two weeks before the raid the couple moved away, and a middle-aged, middle-class couple moved into the house. The police, wearing plain clothes and simulating intoxication, broke into the house at 2 A.M. The husband jumped from bed, grabbed a gun, and shot a policeman. The police shot back. The wife wrenched a gun from another policeman and shot off three of his fingers. Then the lights were turned on and the mistake was discovered. Those who think the "professionalism" of police will prevent abuse have few rivals in their naïveté. Even the most "professional" police departments seldom reprimand such abuses.[20]

The Fifth Amendment to the U.S. Constitution is designed to prevent our government from forcing its citizens to testify

---

[18] A federal court in Washington, D.C. has since voided the arrests and ordered all bail money returned to those arrested.

[19] Columnist Art Buchwald has suggested a humorous alternative he calls the Nixon No Flush Act. It provides ten years and a $10,000 fine for anyone convicted of flushing his toilet after the doorbell rings.

[20] As Gerald Caplan, General Counsel for the Washington, D.C. police department, reported recently: "I do not think we have ever had an officer in the metropolitan police department disciplined for breaching the procedural protections of the Fourth, Fifth, or Sixth Amendments." See, "Crime and Punishment in America," op. cit., p. 17.

against themselves. In order to secure incriminating testimony against some, the practice has been to offer immunity from prosecution to others in exchange for their testimony. Now if one still refuses to testify, he faces, under the Organized Crime Control Act, summary imprisonment for up to three years, without bail or even a trial.

In the 1950s and 1960s the World War II practice of tapping the telephones of foreign embassies was expanded to others. Now the Omnibus Crime Control Act and the new D.C. Court Reform Act have authorized virtually unlimited expansion of electronic surveillance. Federal, state, and local police, with the permission of judges in their jurisdictions, may plant taps and bugs on anyone, in the words of one writer, "who has committed, was committing, or was about to commit crimes punishable by a year or more in prison, or on anyone who was even remotely connected with such suspects."[21] Former Attorney General Mitchell indicated that he would not abide by the Supreme Court rulings in this area and the Justice Department was eavesdropping electronically, *without a court order,* on persons whom Mitchell considered a threat to national security.

The United States has always practiced pretrial detention. Students of the American judicial process estimate that 80 percent of the people in jail are there awaiting trial—and about 35 to 45 percent of them are acquitted when they come to trial.[22] The Bail Reform Act of 1966 attempted to alleviate this repression by establishing a system whereby people were released on their own recognizance. This act helped to make our pretrial processes consistent with the presumption of innocence. But it applied only to federal detention, and the vast majority of arrests occur in states and cities.

Despite such pervasive practice, pretrial detention in noncapital cases has seldom been recognized as legitimate in our system.[23] Under a slightly different twist—preventive detention—the practice of pretrial detention has received the stamp of legitimacy in the D.C. Court Reform Act. It allows a federal

[21] Harris, *op. cit.,* p. 238.

[22] "Crime and Punishment in America," *op. cit.,* p. 40.

[23] There are scattered exceptions, including the internment of striking Wobblies in Bisbee, Arizona in the early part of this century.

judge to detain a person before trial for sixty days if he thinks that person is dangerous to the community.

In America we say one is presumed innocent until proved guilty, but that is not our practice. It is one thing to have a practice that is inconsistent with our ideals and to develop programs like the Bail Reform Act to bring our practices closer to our ideals. It is quite another to use a longstanding illegitimate practice as justification for broadening such a practice and avoiding the ideal. This is precisely what the Nixon administration has done.

This tendency to avoid striving for the ideal and to legitimize the illegitimate practice is reflected in another of the new laws— the "dangerous special offender" section of the Organized Crime Control Act. Title X of this law authorizes a judge to sentence any person convicted of a felony up to twenty-five years if the judge agrees with the prosecutor that the person is a dangerous special offender. As James Bennett, former Director of the U.S. Bureau of Prisons, understated in testimony before the House Judiciary Committee, if this provision had been in effect in the past, at least half of the men in our adult prisons could have been given the twenty-five-year sentence.

Probably the most widespread effect of this provision, one that will be sorely felt in the next decade, will be on the prevalent practice of what is frequently called "negotiated guilt." What typically happens in a criminal case today is that the defendant is charged with multiple offenses for any single alleged act. In exchange for a plea of guilty, prosecutors and judges negotiate with defendants, offering them a charge of only one offense for the single alleged act and offering that their sentences for multiple alleged offenses run concurrently.[24] This is a most common practice, employed in perhaps 85 to 90 percent of all criminal cases in this country. The dangerous special offender provision will increase this problem by providing prosecutors with a potent weapon to use in their attempts to "induce" guilty pleas.[25]

[24] George Cole, "The Decision to Prosecute," *Law and Society Review*, 4, 3 (February 1970), 331–345. Negotiated guilt or "plea copping," as it is more frequently called, is now being legitimized by incorporation into state statute books at the insistence of state crime commissions. This is proceeding under the progressive guise of honestly recognizing the practice.

[25] Other legislation increasing police repression includes authorizing a

Because we are categorizing more behavior as criminal, those who govern are increasingly able to use criminal indictments to counter radical opposition. Political trials are the result.[26] But this form of repression need not rely on the more glamorous laws such as conspiracy or sedition. Orthodox crimes are also used. Sometimes such crimes—theft, arson, fraud—are committed for political purposes, and attempts to punish the crime are motivated by a desire to stymie the political movement or life style of those accused.[27] At other times, no crime has been committed, and the charge reflects a blatant attempt by authorities to frame the defendant. Such attempts are more frequently successful than most care to realize.

The new repressive laws and the political trials that follow them are selective—they are intended to apply to specific types of people in the political system. Most observers are now familiar with the plebeian pattern of selective enforcement that exists. Anachronistic laws are occasionally discovered that prove useful in countering the opposition; traffic enforcement is sometimes selective; and the concerted assault by law enforcement on the Black Panther party and other radicals is clearly so.[28] The same selectivity applies to the new instruments of no-knock, wiretapping, preventive detention, dangerous special offenders, and conspiracy. They

---

practice known as "stop and frisk." The standard necessary for police to search a person on the streets was once "probable cause"—that is, probable cause to believe that a suspect had committed a crime and that he might be armed. Recognizing that police were not observing this standard anyway, state legislatures across the country, spurred on by state and local crime commissions, have established a much lower standard. Now a policeman need only have "reasonable suspicion" as the basis for searching and interrogating a person on the street. Just as with preventive detention, we have legalized previously illegal practices by police.

[26] The best collection of materials to date is Theodore Becker, *Political Trials* (Indianapolis, Ind.: Bobbs-Merrill, 1971). See also Nathan Hakman, "Political Trials and the Legal Order: A Political Scientist's Perspective," *Journal of Public Law* (1972).

[27] Thomas Emerson, "Political Trials," *Law and Social Action* (Winter 1970), p. 6.

[28] Twenty-eight members, chiefly local leaders, of the Black Panther party were killed by policemen in the two-year period ending January 1, 1970. See, Harris, *op. cit.,* p. 250. In 1968 and 1969 there were 750 arrests recorded against members of this party. See Richard Barnet and Marcus Raskin, *An American Manifesto* (New York: Signet, 1970), p. 44.

are applied very selectively. Isn't it significant that there is no use of these instruments to catch corporate criminals, those who rig prices, pharmaceutical firms that dispense potentially harmful drugs, or corporations that discriminate against blacks and women? In commenting on this selectivity, sociologist Troy Duster asks rhetorically, "After our experience with price-fixing in the electrical industry, why don't we use preventive detention against General Electric executives; they are probably hard-core recidivists with respect to collusion and therefore qualify for pretrial detention under the law."[29]

The conclusion to be drawn from the selective criminalization and enforcement is inescapable: laws are passed and applied to control certain groups—the lower economic classes and the most extreme opposition to governmental policy.[30]

Even if the repression by legislators, courts, prosecutors, and police were not increasing, external repression would still be pervasive. The quest for control has resulted in an enormous proliferation of control organizations. Political activities are only one of the objects of control; but, according to the American Civil Liberties Union, at least twenty agencies, at the federal level alone, engage in political surveillance of American citizens. The FBI has 2,000 agents investigating political activities, the Army employs more than 1,200 agents for domestic spying, and the CIA has offices for domestic surveillance in major cities across the country, "often under the cover of commercial umbrellas."[31] This cult of controllers includes numerous other federal agencies in the surveillance game,[32] and the cadre is growing every year. Different components of the federal surveillance network have

---

[29] "Crime and Punishment," *op. cit.,* p. 15.

[30] Jack D. Douglas (ed.), *Crime and Justice in American Society* (Indianapolis, Ind.: Bobbs-Merrill, 1971). See the introduction and his leading essay for a fuller elaboration of this argument. He concludes that "criminal laws are specifically enacted by the middle and upper classes to place the poorer classes under the more direct control of the police, while the middle and upper classes pass only civil laws to control violations within their own ranks." *Ibid.;* pp. xvii–xviii.

[31] David Wise and Thomas B. Ross, *The Invisible Government* (New York: Random House, 1964), p. 350.

[32] Other federal agencies in domestic political surveillance include the National Security Council, the Defense Intelligence Agencies, the National

7 to 15 million political suspects, depending on the agency.[33]

Federal agencies charged with political surveillance responsibilities now have a growing amount of assistance from state
and local intelligence units. These are newly constituted units
of law enforcement whose members are increasingly to be
found as undercover agents on college campuses or in politically active groups in the community at large. The intelligence
unit of the Philadelphia police department has dossiers on
18,000 people and 600 organizations in the area. This pattern
is repeated in city after city all across the country.[34]

Most of these surveillance units were formed since 1960.
Lists and dossiers are coded, computerized, stored, and made
accessible to all branches of the intelligence network.[35] The
FBI is now coordinating the compilation and otherwise acting
as the central repository of the expanding intelligence systems. By 1984 extensive information on hundreds of thousands
of people, including data about their relatives and friends, will
be codified, computerized, and made accessible on a nationwide scale. Even now documents known as "agitator indices"
are developed and circulated to other members of the intelligence community by the FBI. Such albums, for example,
were used by law enforcement in connection with the demonstrations at Resurrection City and at the 1968 Democratic
Convention in Chicago.[36]

It is no longer possible to look only to government as the
source of political surveillance. The new industrial state is an
amalgam of both public and private spheres; were their sepa-
ration not so celebrated in our ideological myths, the distinction would have all but disappeared. The industrial state concept applies not only to military preparedness and to the

Security Agency, Navy Intelligence, Air Force Intelligence, the State Department's Bureau of Intelligence and Research, the Atomic Energy Commission, and various House and Senate committees. Within the last two years
Army surveillance in the state of Illinois included monitoring the behavior
of Senator Adlai E. Stevenson, III, Representative Abner Mikva, and
former Governor Otto Kerner.

[33] Frank Donner, "The Theory and Practice of American Political Intelligence," *New York Review of Books,* April 22, 1971, pp. 27–93.

[34] *Ibid.*

[35] *Ibid.*

[36] *Ibid.* The FBI agent who suggested the idea received a special
commendation.

welfare service component of official enterprises, but to its directly repressive actions as well. For instance, a "private" firm in Dayton, Ohio, known as Agitator Detection, Inc., boasts "complete, computerized files on every known American dissident. . . . And all 160 million of their friends, relatives and fellow travelers."[37]

Lest the reader conclude that repression does not intrude into his life, it should be understood that our actions need not be directly political or criminal to experience harassment, violations of our privacy, and control of our behavior. The intrusion of calculated control, armed with sophisticated technology, is coming from many directions. Credit bureaus provide a demonstrative example. Their basic stock in trade is the accumulation of computerized data on individuals. There are virtually no checks on the reliability of the information included, and the collection proceeds without meaningful concerns for privacy. Members of the Associated Credit Bureaus of America offer their clients a "watch service," which involves "monitoring the public records and an individual's financial transactions after he has been extended credit, in order to inform the lender promptly if there is any indication that the customer will be unable to meet his obligation.[38] Many of the "Welcome Newcomer" programs of towns across America, called "Welcome Wagons" in some locales, are really designed to snoop and report on the characteristics and status of new members of the community to the sponsoring merchants.[39] The Motor Vehicle Bureaus of many states have been selling their information to credit bureaus for decades. Many credit bureaus open their files to law enforcement and other governmental agencies on request. The FBI alone collects from them over 25,000 credit reports annually. It is common for sensitive information held by credit bureaus to be used for noncredit-granting purposes. With the increasing centralization of these record systems, there is every reason to believe that they will be made available to anyone who wishes to monitor an individual's associations, movements,

[37] *Ibid.*

[38] Arthur R. Miller, *The Assault on Privacy* (Ann Arbor: University of Michigan Press, 1971), p. 83.

[39] *Ibid.*, p. 85.

habits, and life style. We are confronted with the possibility of experiencing by 1984, as more sophisticated technology is developed for repressive purposes, a complex hierarchical information network, similar to our telephone system, whose total data base is available to any subscriber. All technological barriers to this have, in fact, already been erased. Many people, not seeking credit, but jobs and dwellings to rent, will be turned down because of information dispersed through this network.

Another serious danger of increasing control and diminution of privacy is evidenced by the tendency toward indiscriminate use of psychological tests, such as personality inventories and those designed to evaluate emotional stability. Personnel managers, both in government and in industry, frequently purport to pass on an individual's "neuroticism," "alienation," "drive," and "stability." As the counter-culture of youth expands, the old culture is simultaneously undergoing a quest for the square American. The Establishment's paranoid exercise of caution is reflected by casting its testing net too wide. An examination of the congressional hearings into the privacy of government employees reveals repeated instances of queries into the most intimate information regarding purely ministerial personnel.[40]

What happens to the responses? At present they are stored in the filing cabinets of personnel departments. Economic considerations and administrative expediency, however, now encourage organizations to maintain machine-based psychological evaluations on their employees. In the near future such considerations will dictate machine storage, with accompanying rapid retrieval. Already proposals for a National Data Center, a repository for all machine-based information about American citizens, have been debated on Capitol Hill. Even without a National Data Center we are sure to see a centralization of record keeping on individuals by the federal government before 1984. There is no question but what the future potential to invade privacy is total, and many of our institutional arrangements and psychological dispositions facilitate it.

If it appears from my analysis to be difficult to be a free man or woman in America today, consider the plight of boys and girls. There exists an array of "juvenile status offenses"

---

[40] *Ibid.,* p. 99

for which an adult would not be legally liable if he committed them. According to the U.S. Children's Bureau, such offenses comprise about 25 percent of the children's cases initially appearing before juvenile courts on a formal petition. Almost half of the young people in state and local detention facilities awaiting an appearance before a juvenile Judge are not charged with crimes, but with special juvenile status offenses. The most common one is being incorrigible. The judges of juvenile courts can mete out harsher sentences for those committing juvenile status offenses than for those who violate criminal statutes.[41]

Not all repression of the young is manifested in promoting criminalization. There are ways to control people other than incarceration or the fear thereof; ill-considered adult chauvinism provides many illustrations. Some of the most visible chauvinistic policies are in our schools. In a recent comprehensive study of American schools, Charles Silberman concludes:

> The public schools . . . are the kind of institution one cannot really dislike until one gets to know them well. Because adults take the schools so much for granted, they fail to appreciate what grim, joyless places most American schools are, how oppressive and petty are the rules by which they are governed, how intellectually sterile and aesthetically barren the atmosphere, what an appalling lack of civility obtains on the part of teachers and principals, what contempt they unconsciously display for children as children.[42]

The rules of schools are incredible. In the typical case, books must be carried in the left hand, all must walk on the right side of the corridor, and written permission from the teacher (telling where the student is going, where he is coming from, and the time to the minute that the pass is valid) is required to be in the halls during class periods.

School administrators promote so much mindless repression partly because they operate on an assumption of distrust. They are likely to trust neither the teachers nor the

[41] A thorough examination of this form of juvenile repression is found in Paul Lerman, "Child Convicts," *Transaction* 8 (July/August, 1971), 35–45.

[42] Charles E. Silberman, "Murder in the Schoolroom," *Atlantic 225* (June 1970), 83. The complete study was published with the title *Crisis in the Classroom* (New York: Random House, 1970).

students, and each of them reciprocates. Many assume that classes are going to be boring places where students will think up facile excuses for avoiding class. Like the society at large, the classroom is turned into a battleground, with each group attempting to outwit the other.

In cases where repression by mindless bureaucratic administration does not deliver copious control, all is not lost. The latest development is to flatten incorrigibility through behavior modification drugs. This practice was first brought to national attention by Robert Maynard in the *Washington Post* in the summer of 1969. He described the practice in Omaha, Nebraska, where between 5 and 10 percent of the 62,000 school children were given drugs "prescribed by local physicians to improve classroom deportment and increase learning potential."[43] Since then numerous articles have appeared and congressional hearings held to discover the extent of the practice and to project its consequences. The frightening picture is painted in neon capsules by Charles Witter, staff director of the congressional committee investigating the matter, writing a book on the subject with the working title of *Big Brother Is a Mother.*

> A careful reading of Department of Health, Education, and Welfare testimony at the . . . hearing suggests that 200,000 children in the United States are now being given amphetamine and stimulant therapy, with probably another 100,000 receiving tranquilizers and antidepressants.
>
> All the experts agree . . . that the use of medication to modify the behavior of grammar school children will radically increase—"zoom" was the word connected with the man most responsible for the promotion of the program at the National Institute of Mental Health. Already specialists in this therapeutic method state that at least 30 percent of ghetto children are candidates, and this figure could run as high as four to six million of the general grammar school population.[44]

Once the practice is established, teachers promote it by identifying the "hyperactive" children, about 70 percent of

[43] Charles Witter, "Drugging and Schooling," *Transaction* 8 (July/August 1971), p. 31.

[44] Reported by Nat Hentoff, "The Drugged Classroom," *Evergreen,* 85 (December 1970), p. 31.

whom are boys, at or above average IQ. The Food and Drug Administration says many of the drugs prescribed are dangerous. They list possible side effects of two drugs in common use: Tofranil = precipitation of glaucoma, difficulty in focusing the eyes, and mild symptoms of Parkinsonism; Aventyl = tremors, internal bleeding, and lowering of blood pressure.[45]

There is every reason to believe this practice will not only be more widespread by 1984, but even more difficult for an individual parent to prevent. The National Education Association's journal, *Today's Education,* reported in January 1969 the conclusion of two professors of education at Indiana University:

> Biochemical and psychological mediation of learning is likely to increase. New drama will play on the educational stage as drugs are introduced experimentally to improve in the learner such qualities as personality, concentration, and memory. The application of biochemical research findings, heretofore centered on infra-human subjects, such as fish . . .[46]

The values of efficiency, conformity, production, and expertise in controlling the decisions regarding children in school are powerful. When Representative Cornelius Gallagher (Democrat, New Jersey), chairman of the Privacy Subcommittee investigating the drugs in school, complained to Congress about the possible dangers of behavior modifying drugs, he was overwhelmed with mail informing him that doctors and teachers know best. His subcommittee was abolished in March 1971.

While new techniques of enforcing adult chauvinism are constantly being developed, its practice and justifications are centuries old. The most common method has been physical punishment. It has been promoted not only to maintain discipline, but also "to transmit educational ideas, to please certain gods or to expel evil spirits."[47] Despite the fact that law enforcement agencies annually report about 10,000 actual cases of child abuse—purposefully inflicted physical injury—

---

[45] *Ibid.,* p. 32.

[46] Quoted in Witter, *op. cit.,* p. 34.

[47] Samuel X. Radbill, "A History of Child Abuse and Infanticide," in Ray E. Helfer and C. Henry Kempe (eds.), *The Battered Child* (Chicago: University of Chicago Press, 1968), p. 3.

and that our best educated guess is that there are between 2.53 and 4.07 million incidents of such abuse in any recent year, there has never been a single nationwide study of the actual incidence of child abuse.[48] We know so little partly because we have not seriously examined the repressive nature of our attitudes toward the little people whose behavior we find relatively easy to control. Extensive parental repression of children should come as no surprise. It is ingrained in our law, which "relegates the child to little more than the status of a chattel." Parents are described as having "property rights in children."[49] Over two hundred years ago Rousseau asked that we "speak less of the duties of children and more of their rights."[50] That we have made no basic changes in either our attitudes or our behavior in at least two centuries should indicate that we are not likely to do so in a decade.

III

A proper understanding of repression and its future requires more than a demonstration that external controls of our conscious behavior have reached an unacceptable level and are increasing. Yet repression is an elusive concept and not one that has received extensive analytical treatment. By repression I am referring to a condition of deprivation in the development of human freedom, resulting from the imposition of controls through the ordering of human activity. There are no simple measures by which to quantify its existence, and, partly for that reason, it has received little attention in analysis. Hence, to appreciate the significance of present trends it

		Objects	
		Conscious	Unconscious
Sources	External	A	B
	Internal	C	D

[48] David G. Gil, "Incidence of Child Abuse and Demographic Characteristics of Persons Involved," Helfer and Kempe (eds.), *op. cit.*, p. 19.

[49] Mary Kohler, "The Rights of Children—An Unexplored Constituency," *Social Policy* 1 (March/April 1971), p. 37.

[50] *Ibid.*

may be useful to distinguish analytically between different types of repression, both in terms of the sources of repression and its objects. As Figure 2 illustrates, repression may stem from external or internal sources. That is, we may be repressed or we may repress ourselves. And it is both our conscious behavior and our unconscious mental processes that may be repressed. Box A depicts the type of repression with which this essay has been most concerned—external conscious repression—and the one that has drawn the attention of most students of politics. This form is more visible than the others. Still we are unable to see just how pervasive it is since it is frequently covert and usually rendered selectively. As I have attempted to show, it is both extensive and growing; much of it is cyclical.

We see it stemming from the jingoism of the immediate post-World War I period and in the strangulation of radical political action during the McCarthy era. And it is reflected in the new repressive laws I have described. Let us not mistake where we are in regard to external (industrial state) policies that repress our conscious behavior: we have further crim-inalized our society; we have greatly expanded political sur-veillance; we have instituted pretrial detention; we have legitimized forced testimony under penalty of imprisonment; we have established no-knock, provision for dangerous special offenders, forced waiver of transactional immunity, and man-datory and harsher sentencing; we have legitimized through law previously illegal practices of police and other state officials; we have provided *agents provocateurs*; we have collected, stored and distributed the most sensitive informa-tion about people; we have drugged elementary school pupils into conformity; and we have shot college demonstrators. With these laws the police need not act illegally for a police state to exist; they need only enforce the laws. Our government can now do virtually anything a police state has ever done, although when it employs this power a bit more subtlety is frequently necessary.

Repression affects our conscious actions, but fully succeeds when it controls us unconsciously. External unconscious re-pression (Box B) is personified by *1984*. Here one is repressed but does not know it. We become so accustomed, "adjusted" some psychologists would say, to external controls of our behavior that such controls become unnecessary. You behave in the "desirable" fashion but do not know why. It is no longer the terror of the club nor the seduction of the drug, but the abandonment of self-determination, the escape from freedom. An extreme manifestation of this was shown by the inmates of concentration camps in Nazi Germany who walked into the gas chambers, knowing they would never return. They did so willingly, with no resistance whatsoever. A quotidian manifestation in modern America is sexual repression. Even though sexual expression is the object of restrictive legislation—statutes even regulating the sexual relations of husband and wife—it is usually limited by invisible customs. Each of us learns to internalize these outside forces. They become second nature to us. We are controlled, but seldom realize it.[51]

Repression, externally imposed on our unconscious mental processes, is closely related to internal or self-repression. But the distinction between them is important. Although they are functionally equivalent and may reinforce one another, the former is manifested in the environment, and the latter in the individual. For this reason internal repression has seldom concerned political scientists, but it is one of many factors that make psychologists necessary. Extensive treatment of its causes and consequences is beyond my competence. However, a few words regarding the interdependence of external and internal repression may help us understand how ominous the problem is. Internal repression is both a conscious and an unconscious process.[52] When it is conscious it reflects our fears of what will happen to us if we do not repress ourselves. It may also reflect the values we use as guides to limit our behavior. In both senses internal conscious repression is

[51] Sexual liberation, however, is underway. Those who identify with the counter-culture are learning to explore their sexual potentials and to overthrow the externally imposed restraints on their sexuality. Gay liberation organizations and women's liberation groups are legitimizing these freedoms. They are not only openly recognizing the externally imposed repressive forces within themselves, they are organizing to communicate to others the extent of sexual repression. (In the summer of 1970 20,000 people marched up Fifth Avenue in New York City to support Gay Liberation.)

[52] Internal unconscious repression is a complex process about which even psychologists admit to knowing little.

directly related to outside forces that socialize our behavior. This can be illustrated by examining the assumptions that underlie parental methods of controlling the behavior of children.

Aggressive, antisocial behavior in children is redirected by parents in one of two ways: either by "fear-oriented" techniques (physical punishment or deprivation of privileges and *things* desired) or "love-oriented" techniques. By using love-oriented techniques parents rely on the common values they have promoted between themselves and their child. The child is made to realize that he has lost parental approval, and he thereby feels guilty and fears losing parental love. Children experiencing fear-oriented techniques may behave appropriately, but only because they wish to avoid being punished, not because they value appropriate behavior. When they think they can get away with it they may offend others because they have not learned to value being inoffensive. When children accustomed to love-oriented techniques refuse to behave offensively it is because they value not hurting others, not because they fear punishment. The value is not absolute, of course, but they have learned to repress themselves. A love-oriented approach thereby reduces external repression by promoting certain values and by minimizing fear in interpersonal relations.[53]

The institutional forces that promote external repression are based on the same assumptions about human behavior that justify fear-oriented techniques in dealing with children. The term "Big Brother" in *1984* is more than a symbolic expression of the state as a family of togetherness.

Properly understood, repression is a manifold phenomenon. It permeates every institution—the family, the school, the corporation, and the government; and in varying degrees, every individual from birth to death. But repression may no longer (if it ever could) be challenged as only an external force.

The problem today and the problem tomorrow is that the distinction between the internal and external sources of repression has been erased, since what now plays the part of

[53] Credit should be given to Philip Slater, *The Pursuit of Loneliness* (Boston: Beacon Press, 1970), who elaborates this example.

internal or self-repression is the external in disguise.[54] This is not to say that no one recognizes external repression. I am more concerned with those who have so internalized external repression that they no longer think they are repressed. They argue that the limits they place on their behavior are independent of external forces. Actually, external repression has become redundant for them in proportion to the degree of coercive control exerted by internal processes. Freedom for them has become a distant, spiritual quality and, like most other spiritual qualities in their life, not a guide to everyday existence.

IV

Repression need not be all encompassing. We can choose the future, for events and institutions that exercise control over us are not omnipotent. They are powerful forces in our inheritance, and they limit our short-run potentials. But our performance can approximate our potentials. It is necessary to reduce the dissociation between our actions and our thoughts about what our actions should be. Most of our actions have predictable consequences; we are, therefore, responsible for them.

To approximate our potentials and significantly reduce repression will require far more effort than presently seems probable. Exhausted by the demands of everyday life and infected with the fear that results from political polarization, middle America seems to have relinquished its future to whatever leadership exists. Many of those whose immediate interest demands drastic change have turned inward and refrained from developing a strategy to meet their needs. This cannot last long. While many individuals are undergoing enormous personal change, the basic structural features of society persist and will not be overcome by 1984. In fact the repressive tools to promote obedience to this structure will be sharpened. Yet I am convinced that society will experience more change in the remainder of this century than it has in the last several

[54] In addition to the many works by Herbert Marcuse, a recent book by Henri Lefebvre, *Everyday Life in the Modern World* (London: Penguin, 1971), should be consulted. See especially Chapter 4, Terrorism and Everyday Life," pp. 143–193.

centuries, and perhaps even throughout history to date. We may lose all our freedom, or we may adjust impending forces in such a way that we will regain certain freedoms lost, even experience new ones. A clear lesson of the 1960s is that leadership and the nature of events can change rapidly. New groups become politically conscious; new issues and movements burst forth and command the moral energies of masses of people. Yet any projection of the future must be based on present trends, not future potentials. With that in mind, 1984 America does not appear to be a happy place.

The best that present trends reveal is a twofold, potentially conflicting transformation of power. The first involves a dissolution rather than a seizure of power and is evidenced by a decay in the power of certain repressive forces. A bare-toothed tiger made of paper promotes little fear. And it is just such an attitude about state power that is growing today. For example, more and more young people are rejecting the institution of marriage; they live together as they wish in open defiance of prohibitive statutes. Some of the factories in the Detroit area have hired permanent part-time employees because of the high absentee rates on Friday and Monday, indicating, I think, the extent to which the work ethic and its enforcers are being rejected by some elements of the American working class. In the short run these alienated elements will reject, in limited ways, any group that is likely to capture power. They don't care about power any more.

Second, there is an emerging, potentially national leadership with the courage to confront the future and work for a fundamental change of direction. The prototype is the few towns and cities where this has happened, the most well-known of which is Berkeley, California. The likelihood that such leadership will capture the presidency within the coming decade is small if not remote; but it can become a real possibility. The young, women who recognize their own exploitation, blacks, Puerto Ricans, Chicanos, poor whites, and more and more members of the middle class are developing not only political consciousness, but political maturity. Political activists of the 1960s who haven't rejected all organized life are more willing to organize strategically than ever before. They understand that a president committed to doing so could change the direction of this country. But not much more should be expected from any one presidential term. We could erase many of the new repressive laws by 1984, but we will not overcome the class basis of legislation. Even if we could, the most repressive features of modern American life are not found in a handful of statutes. Repression is more deeply rooted than the actions of police who enforce class law.

The maintenance of repression is a fundamental consequence of certain constants, which any aspiring politician is not likely to defy and which personal anarchism does not challenge. These include the distribution of income and power, the burgeoning population and resultant urban density, the constant growth of the economy, and the expansion of bureaucracy.

Since much of the repression in American life is class based, a reduction of the radically unequal distribution of wealth and power is a necessary condition of lessening the repression stemming from this source. No significant trend toward income equality has appeared in this century.[55] Even the impact of federal income taxes on the actual distribution of wealth has been minimal, if not insignificant.[56] Hence, the class basis of legislation and the role of police in enforcing class law will likely continue to enforce usually latent, but occasionally open, class warfare.

Another constant contributing to modern repression is population growth and urban density. The population of our country grew 250 percent in the first two-thirds of the twentieth century. During the last third we can expect an addition of as many as were added in the first two-thirds. Most of this growth has been and will continue to be in the cities, for nearly all rural areas are losing population. This promotes multitudinous incidents of repression. The increase and the migration of the black population between 1960 and 1970, for example, has meant a 20 percent increase in the public school enrollment of black children. And the crowding of ghetto schools has turned many of them into veritable prisons.

[55] The most extensive examination of this question is in Gabriel Kolko, *Wealth and Power in America* (New York: Praeger, 1962.) He demonstrates that the total income share of the richest tenth of the population has dropped only slightly, if at all, since 1910. Yet the two lowest income-tenths have experienced a sharp decline in the past half a century.

[56] *Ibid.,* p. 30.

This population density has brought more blacks under the direct control of police. Presently, "two-thirds of all arrests take place among only about two percent of the population."[57] And we all know who they are and where they live. Both crime and police repression increase in proportion to the expansion of the population of the ghetto, not the lesser population increase of the society at large. There is every reason to believe that population and urban density will continue to increase. The repression they produce will increase as well.

Repression is also a result of our policy of continued economic growth—a policy that few challenge. However, economic growth comes with a high price in hidden costs, one of which is an increase in crime and a corresponding increase in repression. Changes in the theft rate, for example, are influenced by economic conditions. In fact, the "increases in crime in recent years are more related to an expanding economy than to a breakdown in human integrity or to a collapse of the moral order."[58] The amateurs who steal today, as distinguished from the professionals more characteristic of the 1930s, are influenced by their sense of deprivation. They steal things they want, but cannot afford. Commodities are their fetish. This occurs not when things they steal are scarce in society, but when they are abundant.[59] We will continue to have increases in property crimes "until we either place less importance on accumulating material possessions or more equitably distribute these possessions throughout society."[60] As our economy grows, bringing more and more affluence to the middle and upper classes, property (read: class) crime by the lower classes will increase as well. If our historical approach to dealing with this phenomenon is any guide to policy makers, our society's response to increasing property crime will not be a more rational distribution of wealth, but a more efficient police repression.

Economic expansion in a class society results in increases in property crimes, which precipitate increases in the repression by police forces; but economic growth produces repres-

[57] Clark, *op. cit.*, p. xi.

[58] Leroy C. Gould, "Crime and Its Impact in an Affluent Society," in Douglas, *op. cit.*, p. 118.

[59] *Ibid.*, p. 112.

[60] *Ibid.*, p. 118.

sion in other ways. Coupled with an expanding population, economic growth in an industrial state broadens bureaucracy, public and private. There is no other way to facilitate the present goals of the industrial system—expansion of production and increases in consumption.

The characteristics of bureaucracy are centralization of authority and responsibility, specialization of work, de-emphasis of the individual person (though not his skills), cult of efficiency, advancement of technology, and secrecy of decision making. If the future of our society is ruled by the goals of the industrial system, then more and more of our everyday life will be spent in service to the characteristics of a bureaucratic order. When the power of the state sustains this political paradigm, the individual becomes dispensable. The structure of society does not serve his needs, he serves the needs of society—bureaucracy, technology, and the expanding economy. The foundations for this life have been laid, some of them quite visibly. The Social Security Amendments of 1971 require that by 1974 recipient mothers with children three years old and older will be required to register to work. The Family Assistance Plan of the Nixon administration contains a most inclusive provision to force people to register to work.

The move from forced work registration of the lower classes (in itself repressive) to forced work by the lower classes is perhaps easier than we might think. The transition is subtle, but devastating. Already our attachments to values of efficiency in ordering social relations incline many of us in this direction. This potential form of nearly total repression is enhanced by our belief in and commitment to the efficaciousness of experts. Conservatives and liberals alike seem enamored with expertise. The increase of specialized knowledge in every domain and reliance on science and technology to solve problems of human behavior have fundamentally altered the pursuit of the ideal of freedom. If it seems doubtful that experts can and will propose that forced work programs are needed, consider the following two cases of proposed behavior modification:

1. Dr. Arnold Hutschnecker, formerly President Nixon's internist, devised a plan to require all six-to-eight-year-olds in the nation to take a predictive psychology test for their criminal potential. Those who flunked the test—which is presumed to be reliable in 50 percent of the cases—would be sent to "rehabilitation centers"

as Hutschnecker phrased it "in a romantic setting with trees out West." This proposal was sent on White House stationery to the Secretary of Health, Education and Welfare requesting suggestions on how it could be implemented. When it was discovered on Capitol Hill only *one* congressional voice—Cornelius Gallagher— was stirred to comment. When he branded the centers "American Dachaus" and requested congressional hearings, the White House dropped the idea.[61]

2. Joseph Meyer, a computer specialist employed by the National Security Agency, has devised a scheme for attaching miniature electronic devices to criminals and other suspect citizens and keeping track of them by computers. The details of the "Crime Deterrent Transponder System" were published in the January, 1971 issue of *Transactions on Aerospace and Electronic Systems.* Meyer proposed that the transponders be attached to twenty million "subscribers" as a condition of bail or parole. A sub- scriber would be identified by a unique code which would be relayed every few seconds to a central computer through a net- work of transceivers set up like police call-boxes in given neighborhoods. The computer would compare the subscribers location with a storage file indicating his permissible movements. Transponders could not be removed without the computer's knowledge; those who did remove them would be charged with a felony. As Meyer described it, "The aim of the transponder surveil- lance scheme is to constrain criminals and arrestees into behaving like law-abiding citizens. If this aim is fulfilled, the subscribers would do ordinary things like get up in the morning and go to work. At night they will stay close to home, to avoid being impli- cated in crimes. At their place of work, a human surveillance system will operate. Low-powered transceivers in their domiciles can monitor them indoors. . . . A transponder surveillance system can surround the criminal with a kind of externalized conscience —an electronic substitute for the social conditioning, group pres- sures, and inner motivation which most of the society lives with . . . many criminals and miscreants seem to have little desire to go along with the social norms, so an externalized control system may be necessary to them, like a heart pacer to a cardiac patient." Meyer thinks his system would cost about $2 billion a year. To minimize the cost to the government he suggests that transponders be leased to subscribers at five dollars a week. And he adds, "In the case of juveniles, it might be necessary to find work for them so they could meet the payments." A version of this scheme has already been tested on a number of volunteers—offenders and mental patients in Boston—by Ralph and Robert Schwitzgebel,

[61] Witter, *op. cit.,* p. 31.

the former having both a law degree and a doctorate in psychology. Truly an expert, promoting an expert's plan![62]

These are not the plans of mad scientists, cloistered in some ivory tower and isolated from policy makers. They are experts, employed by the federal government to construct plans to be translated into policy. They assist in programming the policies of official control organizations, whose autonomy and power is constantly being enhanced by relying on the status of "scientific experts." The image of expertise is not limited to the advisors. The line officer in law enforcement is able to assume greater and greater amounts of discretion by being imbued with the image of being a "professional police-man." In fact, few groups operate in greater secrecy; a secrecy enhanced as policemen become more isolated from civilian pressures by becoming more professional.[63] Any disregard for the liberties of citizens tends to be shielded by the power of police to "investigate" themselves when complaints are lodged against them. No one else, police organizations tell us, is professionally qualified to do so. The more such groups are able to remove themselves from democratic controls and embrace so-called "professional" status, the more precarious is the status of our individual liberties, and the more they can argue that repression is simply efficiency.[64]

We must anticipate the further expansion of professional repression, of more efficient, legally sanctioned, widely accepted, and technologically sophisticated attempts to program what we do and what we learn to do, our conscious and our unconscious. The trends in this direction are too pervasive and too well-entrenched to avoid in the short-run of ten or fifteen years. Those who recognize these trends and respond to them by attempting to avoid all contact with the culture out of which they grow should also anticipate being overpowered by those whose existence they hope to deny. A repressive culture can swallow another, destroy the acquiescent and itself.

[62] See Robert Barkan's report, "Big Brother," *Ramparts,* September 1971, pp. 10–12.

[63] William A. Westley, *Violence and the Police* (Cambridge, Mass.: MIT Press, 1970), pp. 110–152.

[64] The Presidential Commission on Violence warned in 1969 that the police were emerging as a "self-conscious, independent political power rivaling even duly elected officials in influence."

ROBERT T. NAKAMURA

is currently an Acting Instructor in Political Science at the University of California, Berkeley, and has also taught American government at San Francisco State College. His field of concentration is the relationship of institutional characteristics to public policy choices at the state and federal levels.

congress confronts the presidency*

Preface to Prediction

It is the dream of every social scientist to be like Hari Selden in Isaac Asimov's science fiction *Foundation* series. Selden used the techniques of psychohistory to predict the history of the future. By applying the known fundamental rules of human behavior to large populations, whose size cancelled out individual vagaries, he was able to write an accurate future history, which in turn became a map for individual action. Selden was a sort of super-Karl Marx.

Prediction for science fiction writers typically consists of extrapolating the significant trends of the present well into the future. Ignatius Donnelly, in *Caesar's Column,* gave us his

* My thanks for many helpful comments and suggestions to Jeffrey L. Pressman, Arnold J. Meltsner, Aaron B. Wildavsky, Gene S. Poschman, Robert Paul Wolff, Frank Thompson, and William Lunch.

vision of the full consequences of increased concentration of wealth and industrialization. Edward Bellamy, in *Looking Backward,* drew a happier picture of technology—presenting the reader with a benevolently managed society. Orwell projected the use of modern technology by dictators into an all-pervasive state. In science fiction the world of institutions is malleable; societies are directly shaped by the writer's sense of important trends.

When the focus of prediction shifts from the trends of science fiction writers to guesses about the future shape of institutional relations, the characteristic inertia of institutions tends to dampen judgments of extensive change. The reason for this is simple. Institutions have a life of their own; they possess an internal stability that is in part insulated from the changing world and in part resting upon the strongest elements of the environment. For example, the House of Representatives distributes its internal power by means of a seniority system. This system satisfies the institutional need for stable, trained career personnel.[1] Changes in personnel, arising out of the previous congressional election, are rarely directly reflected in major shifts of internal power. The electoral base for the seniority system is founded upon the stable party identifications and loyalties of voters in numerous "safe districts." It is possible for major changes to occur in a society without directly and immediately affecting the political arrangement of such institutions.

Because institutions are by nature insulated from the world, predictions about their future are not necessarily accomplished by linking events directly to institutional futures. To a large extent, an understanding of the future shape of relations between Congress and the presidency comes with an appreciation of their capacity to insulate themselves from changes in the world. Since the House of Representatives has been characterized as the most insensitive of the major institutions, it will be used as the example of how an institution can dampen the effect of substantial outside change. On the

---

[1] Nelson W. Polsby, Miriam Gallagher, and Barry Rundquist, "The Growth of the Seniority System in the U.S. House of Representatives," *The American Political Science Review* 63 (September 1969), 787–807.

other hand, an example of major institutional change is the breach of the presidential monopoly over foreign policy—and the attendant increase in senatorial activity.

This essay is divided into three general sections. The first deals with the circumstances and characteristics of institutional change. It seeks to explain the shift from a strong foreign policy president, free to enact and enforce commitments, to a president who will have to compete with institutional rivals. This example specifies some of the ways in which recent political experiences are translated into changes in the balance of institutional powers. The second section demonstrates the ability of an institution—the House of Representatives—to dampen the effects of outside change. The third section is reserved for guesses about the form of future political conflicts between Congress and the presidency.

The Post-Vietnam Presidency

Within recent memory, presidents have pursued their foreign policies with varying degrees of freedom. Prior to World War II, FDR's freedom of action was severely constrained by isolationist sentiments within the public, Congress, and interest groups.[2] By contrast, LBJ enjoyed enough discretion to commit the nation to war over a two-year period with only the slightest opposition. Both FDR and LBJ enjoyed the same formal powers under the Constitution: the command of the armed forces, the responsibility for the conduct of foreign relations, and so on. The differences in their effective power can be explained, in part, by several factors: the climate of public opinion, the level of interest-group competition, and the strength and will of congressional rivals. As the reaction to the Vietnam war sets into the fabric of American politics, these factors are again undergoing change. An examination of the ways in which these changes are translated into the strengthening and weakening of institutional powers can give

---

[2] James McGregor Burns, *Roosevelt: The Lion and the Fox* (New York: Harcourt Brace Jovanovich, 1956), Chapter 13, "Foreign Policy by Makeshift," pp. 247–263.

us an outline of the shapes being assumed by the post-Vietnam presidency and Congress.

Our Transient Loyalties: Changing Climate of Opinion

The most enduring partisan alignments in American politics seem to be those separated by the question: Whose ox is being gored? People who care about political outcomes often change their mind about institutions. The virtue of a position depends on who gets what, when, where, and how. Nowhere is the truth of this simple assertion more evident than in the transient loyalties of political actors to the standard institutional forms: the Supreme Court, Congress, and the presidency. Activists and even academics love or despise institutions according to their felt needs at the time—the judiciary is viewed differently if it is the "horse and buggy" court of "nine old men" frustrating the New Deal or the progressive Warren Court expanding the effective rights of racial minorities and the poor. Our relative affection for Congress and the presidency varies similarly with circumstances. Frequently, support for the one is in inverse proportion to the other. There is really nothing wrong with such fluid loyalties; after all, *The Federalist Papers* remind us that is the way things are supposed to work in a system of checks and balances.

From the New Deal through the early sixties, the presidency was at its zenith in popularity among liberals. Presidents presided over the expansion of the welfare state at home and pursued internationalist policies abroad. Meanwhile, Congress parsimoniously checked necessary governmental spending and resisted the assumption of modern international obligations. It seemed that executives could do no wrong and Congress very little right. This disposition of heroes and villains came to an abrupt end with the Indochina war. The president remains strong, but it is no longer a wholly benevolent strength. The cry is for a more assertive Congress, but "the power of the purse and the sword" seems to have grown somewhat rusty from disuse. The moral of this is that opinions change and changes are caused by shifts in issues of importance which cast an institution in a particular light.

A New Dominant Metaphor:
Vietnam for Munich

Such shifts of elite and popular affection do not occur out of thin air. They are caused by the translation of important events into political lessons. Explanations of major political events give the public, Congress, and president basic categories—appropriate or inappropriate—with which to explain and evaluate future events. Disenchantment with World War I, focusing on the undesirability of foreign involvement, laid the foundation for isolationism, which proved to be an important constraint on FDR's handling of foreign affairs prior to Pearl Harbor. The Munich analogy, with its lessons about the costs of appeasement, had a vitality into the sixties, when it was used to explain and justify Vietnam. To some extent, the impact of each of these events is temporary. But temporary is a long time in American politics.

It must be apparent that elements of the Indochina war are going to provide the major parts of the dominant metaphor for the popular understanding of foreign policy until the next cataclysmic event. However, the lessons of such major events are rarely direct. Political occurrences are much too complex for such direct analogy and the public is too inattentive for direct absorption of such lessons. In order for this series of events to become hardened into political lessons, at least a couple of things must occur. First, a connection must be drawn between the events themselves so that the resulting story clarifies the lessons and morals. Second, these explanations must find political and institutional means for their expression. If the lessons of Vietnam become as compelling as the Munich analogy, then the relative power of Congress and the presidency in the conduct of foreign affairs will be changed.

The Recent Past

The period between the end of World War II and the middle of the Vietnam war was a good time for the exercise of presidential power in foreign affairs. Aaron B. Wildavsky has pointed out that executive power during this time was essentially bifurcated by issue area: a strong foreign policy president and a relatively weak domestic leader.[3] The presidential record of success in behalf of liberal domestic proposals was spotty: Truman's frequent defeats by Congress, JFK's lack of success in medicare, aid to education, and so on. The major exception, LBJ, owes his success to the catastrophic defeat of Barry Goldwater, which yielded lopsided Democratic majorities in the House of Representatives. Contrasting with this routine of failure in domestic affairs is the almost unbroken chain of presidential foreign policy victories: United States entry into the United Nations, Marshall Plan, NATO, Truman Doctrine, Korea, nuclear test-ban treaty, decision to enter Vietnam, invasions of the Dominican Republic, Cambodia, and Laos. The very Congresses which voted down presidential domestic legislation and gutted appropriations for social programs usually quiescently voted massive appropriations for defense and war.

This contrast of strength and weakness between the foreign and domestic presidencies derives from differences between the two issue areas in four categories: first, varying amounts of formal power to act; second, the climate of opinion; third, the level of interest-group competition; and fourth, the strength and will of congressional rivals. In domestic affairs the president often lacks the ability to order things to happen; he may face a hostile public, interest groups may oppose him, and congressmen may have alternative plans of action. The recent wage and price freeze provides an example of some of these factors. President Nixon took his initial action on a congressional grant of authority; many elements of his program required additional powers that awaited legislative action. Subsequently, he has had to reconcile his labor and congressional critics. Presidential powers in economic matters are those explicitly granted by Congress, those that adhere to his administrative control of the federal bureaucracy, and to his ability to sway public opinion. In exercising this bundle of powers, he is often opposed by strong interest groups and elements in Congress.

In the recent past this situation contrasted sharply with the president's freedom in foreign policy. He enjoyed substantial

[3] Aaron B. Wildavsky, "The Two Presidencies," *Transaction* 4 (December 1966), 7–14.

power, associated with being commander in chief and chief diplomat, that allowed him to create de facto situations. Like Teddy Roosevelt, his successors have had the ability to send the Great White Fleet "halfway around the world"—then to rely on Congress to appropriate the money to get them back. His potential rivals—Congress, interest groups, and the public —either by choice or necessity have hitherto lacked the will or resources to successfully prevent presidential action. These are the underpinnings of presidential foreign policy hegemony that are now being shaken.

Changes in Presidential Strength

The president's formal and effective powers in foreign affairs are considerable and have been recently quite sacred. Conversely, the formal power of his principal rival, Congress, has gone largely unexercised. Although it is inconceivable that the roles of the sixties will ever be totally reversed with a strong foreign policy Congress and weak president (as in the period preceding the War of 1812), some change in the relative balance of power is highly likely. This process falls into two general parts: first, an undermining in the faith in, or desirability of, presidential control; and second, an increase in aggressiveness of presidential rivals. The first involves such things as a changing conception of the national interest, decreased faith in the president's principal resources of knowledge and command. The second seeks to explain increased activity on the part of rivals, principally the Senate. In short, the climate of opinion that supported presidential hegemony is changing, as is the willingness of his rivals to compete for control.

The president enjoyed control of foreign policy during the fifties and sixties partially because his rivals conceded that he ought to exercise control. Although many things explain this abdication, several reasons have been selected for examination. There was the postwar consensus on the anticommunist goals of American policy. As long as everyone agreed on goals, the only real question was implementation. The president was best equipped to implement goals due to his superior command of information and role as head of the armed forces. His information was thought to be good, and American arms and resources sufficient to any task.

Changing Conception of National Interest

The reservation of foreign affairs as an executive preserve
is linked to the notion of a public interest. The concept of a
public interest, a doctrine long out of fashion in the domestic
politics of large industrial societies, until recently has survived unchallenged as the touchstone of foreign relations:
the national interest.

Once the clarity of a national interest becomes established
the only relevant concerns are those of speed and efficiency
—things that favor the seemingly concentrated power of
the executive over the obviously dispersed power of the legislature. With occasional exceptions—notably during the
McCarthy era—Congress, the Supreme Court, and sporadic
opinion polls endorsed this view through the early sixties.
This notion took various forms: "bipartisan" foreign policy
during the fifties and the "technical question" arguments
made in defense of Vietnam decisions. As Senator Ervin said:

> The President . . . has the advantage of the intelligence received
> by him from the intelligence sources on the scene in South
> Vietnam. He also has the advantage of the advice of men who
> have spent their lives studying military matters.[4]

The idea that the only difference between senators and presidents was the level of information, given the same conception
of the national interest, led President Johnson to opine: "If
you knew what I know, then you would be acting in the same
way." The assumptions that support the national interest view
—that there is a single and determined interest and that the
president is best equipped to act on it—are now under
intensive scrutiny.

The settled consensus after World War II had been that the
spread of communism was against the national interest. Subscribers to this view included many informed and uninformed
segments of the public and most elected officials. At times
the specific formulation of this national interest caused some
differences in emphasis. Some Midwestern legislators were

[4] Quoted in Eugene P. Dvorin (ed.), *The Senate's War Powers: Debate on
Cambodia from the Congressional Record* (Chicago: Markham, 1971), p. 79.

most concerned with Asian communism, responding to the success of the communist revolution in China, while others from the Northeast emphasized European difficulties and solutions like the Marshall Plan, aid to Greece, and NATO. While specific areas of concern differed, the consensus on the national interest remained constant—the spread of communism had to be checked. As long as there was an agreement on foreign policy goals, the only question centered around implementation.

Since Vietnam, the national consensus has evaporated into a dissensus; there is substantial disagreement where previously there had been agreement. While subscribers to the theory of monolithic communism remain, their arguments are disputed by others who point out that communism can be as pluralistic as anything else. In addition to disagreement among older foreign policy elites, within Congress and the academies, new participants have mobilized due to the war and the emergence of attentive issue-publics. Many of these new participants are unfamiliar with the cold war socialization experience of their elders. The current dissensus on the national interest has a number of causes, many of which will be explored later. One important reason for the differing views of communism might be tied to reality. During the postwar years, the Soviet Union was the preeminent communist nation, and the rest were literally or apparently satellites. Naturally the concentration of communist power in the Soviet Union, and within Russia in Stalin, lent itself to the view of monolithic communism. The emergence of independent communist nations such as China and Cuba—supplementing Yugoslavia—has contributed to a more pluralistic conception on the part of many. The Sino-Soviet split and the internecine contentiousness of many communist leaders have furthered this notion. Thus for a variety of reasons—changed circumstances, different opinions, new participants unencumbered by cold war ideological baggage—the previous consensus on the national interest has given way to disagreement. As conceptions of interest widen, the president's arguments about his technical superiority wane. The executive and his potential rivals no longer agree on goals. Simultaneously, there has been a growth in doubts about the capacity of the presidency to make foreign policy, unencumbered by rivals. To state the obvious, the simple-minded faith in the technical competence of the president to make and execute foreign policy decisions has been seriously undermined by the war. Under conditions of intense scrutiny and increased demands, any political organization is going to be hard put to perform satisfactorily. The presidency has not been an exception. As more and more segments of the public and Congress monitor presidential successes and failures—using diverse and conflicting criteria —it is only natural that such close scrutiny yields information of shortcomings. In the past, many believed that the president should be left alone in foreign affairs and he would do a good job, but such faith is no longer automatic.

Recent experiences have weakened popular and congressional acceptance of presidential hegemony in foreign affairs. Widening and competing conceptions of the national interest have diminished ready acceptance of presidential leadership. The Indochina war has demonstrated that the circle of presidential decision makers was perhaps too narrow, and such narrowness worked to foreclose alternative policies. This perception of narrowness undermined congressional faith in the completeness of the information released to them, as well as their confidence in the adequacy of presidential councils. Furthermore, the course of the war has shaken another foundation of presidential hegemony—the belief that American might could triumph where judgment may have failed.

Small Circle of Friends

In retrospect, it is apparent that the sheer concentration of decision-making power in the White House—especially during the early stages of the Vietnam war—kept the relevant alternatives constrained to variations of supporting an anticommunist government in Saigon.[5] The narrowness of these alternatives, due in large part to the limited circle of relevant actors, laid the foundation for later mistakes. President Johnson could keep the circle small, usually to people who agreed with him, and still have the confidence that he could enforce his policy choices on Congress and the nation. *When*

[5] Eugene Eidenberg, "The Presidency: Americanizing the War in Vietnam," in Allan P. Sindler (ed.), *American Political Institutions and Public Policy* (Boston: Little, Brown, 1969), pp. 68–126.

*these decisions soured, there were very few to share the
blame. Concentration of power means concentration of
responsibility.*

In the past, the centralization of power was said to promote effectiveness by facilitating speed and decisiveness in
action. There are increasing doubts about the desirability of
such concentration of power. Former presidential press secretary George Reedy likened the White House to a monarch's
court, where sycophants and courtiers triumphed over
advisors by reinforcing the monarch's decided preferences.[6]
Even where dissent was heard in presidential circles, its purpose seemed more to legitimize the decided action than to
alter it:

> . . . within these councils (on Vietnam) there was always at
> least one "devil's advocate." But an official dissenter always
> starts with half his battle lost. It is assumed that he is bringing
> up arguments solely because arguing is his official role. It is
> well understood that he is not going to press his points harshly
> or stridently. Therefore, his objections and cautions are dis-
> counted before they are delivered. They are actually welcomed
> because they prove for the record that decision was preceded
> by controversy.[7]

The weakness of the system, as Reedy and others argue, lies
in the fact that the president only hears his subordinates; and
frequently that is the same thing as hearing what he wants to
hear. There are probably some genuine advantages to a more
competitive situation. Reedy sketches the Senate as an
example:

[6] If there were a musical written about presidential advisors, one of the
songs could be: "I'm just a boy who can't say no." To some extent
Reedy's complaints may be generic to advisors of powerful men. Albert
Speer wrote:

> There is a special trap for every holder of power, whether the director
> of a company, the head of a state, or the ruler of a dictatorship. His
> favor is so desirable to his subordinates that they will sue for it by
> every means possible. Servility becomes endemic among his entourage,
> who compete among themselves in their show of devotion. This in
> turn exercises a say upon the ruler, who becomes corrupted in his
> turn. [*Inside the Third Reich* (New York: Avon 1970), p. 127.]

Advisors to real princes, like Machiavelli and Thomas More, said pretty
much the same thing.

[7] George Reedy, *The Twilight of the Presidency* (Cleveland: World Publish-
ing, 1970), p. 11.

My own heart is back in the Senate. . . . This is not because
the people at the other end of Pennsylvania Avenue are any
better in terms of character, wisdom, or goals. It is simply that
their egos must face daily clashes with similarly strong egos
who stand on a par and who do not feel any sense of subordina-
tion. In the Senate, no course stands the remotest chance of
adoption unless a minimum of fifty-one egotistical men are per-
suaded of its wisdom. . . . These are preconditions under which
even the most neurotic of personalities must make some
obeisance to reality.[8]

Since power is much more concentrated in foreign affairs, the
weaknesses of concentration are seen as much greater. The
preceding does not argue that presidential decision making is
fatally flawed; that would be absurd. Rather, the notion that
foreign policy decisions are best left entirely to the president
—because hierarchical councils are most productive—is
undergoing revision. That in itself is enough to encourage
and legitimize disagreements between representatives and
presidents on foreign policy questions. In politics, the actual
technical superiority or inferiority of a system of decision
making is less important than elite and public perceptions of
those things.

George Reedy and many others are making an argument
about power that has been very persuasive in American politics. They say that concentration of power breeds a weakness
in decisions. When presidents no longer have to contend with
objections and competition from other powerful men, executives can lose touch with the actual and practical limitations
on their own power. James Madison warned against concentration of political power as breeding tyranny, still others
warn against concentration of industrial power because it
breeds lower-level consumer products. For a variety of reasons, arguments against the concentration of power in a
single hand find resonance among elites.

Accusations of narrowness strike hard at the basis of presidential strength. When his rivals think that the President's
circle of advisors is too narrow and too uniform, then respect
for the wisdom of executive deliberations declines. Congressmen are less respectful of occasional information releases by
the executive if they believe that arguments have already been

[8] *Ibid.,* pp. xiii–xiv.

filtered by special pleaders. The result of such a development may be that the president will have to deal more frequently and candidly with the other egotists on Capitol Hill.

The Faith in Power

Another element of undermined confidence in the executive branch is the newly aroused distrust, or disappointment, in the military. An unarticulated assumption had been that the president by sheer military power could enforce his decisions —faith in the military as an instrument was an important underpinning of faith in presidential leadership in foreign affairs. In the realpolitik conception of foreign policy, the right decisions are the successful ones, and success depends on power.[9] Due to political limitations imposed by the president on the military, the inviability of South Vietnam as an ally, inexperienced with guerrilla warfare, as well as overconfident predictions, confidence in the American military has been severely hurt by Indochina. These injuries manifest themselves in a number of ways: internal difficulties in the Army, closer congressional scrutiny of military appropriations, disenchantment of the president and Congress with military estimates. Presidents will be constricted in their future decisions by a tighter notion of the possible now that the limits of military capacity have been clarified by the Vietnam experience. Such a sense of limits will continue to act as a constraint into the next decade.

The cumulative effect of competing conceptions of a national interest in foreign relations and increased doubts about the presidential ability to make sound decisions and successfully enforce his choices may all be temporary byproducts of the Vietnam war. In order for these newly discovered shortcomings and lessons to be incorporated into

---

[9] Irving Louis Horowitz said of the Pentagon Papers that they reveal many items of ignorance including:

". . . the unanticipated arrogance of assuming throughout that logistics would conquer all. Even the doves like George W. Ball never doubted for a moment that an influx of a certain number of United States troops would in fact swing the tide of battle the way that General Westmoreland said it would." ["The Pentagon Papers and Social Science," *Transaction 8* (September 1971), p. 42.]

a shift of institutional powers, between the president and his congressional rivals, linkages must be established.

Distrust of, or disappointment with, presidential power in foreign affairs is not a totally sufficient hedge to presidential initiatives. After all, the president as commander in chief still has the power to present Congress with a *fait accompli* such as the invasion of Laos—or, for that matter, World War III. Furthermore, the president's wide discretion allows him to interpret congressional action as he chooses—for instance, viewing the prohibition against the use of ground troops in Laos as excluding helicopter pilots and intelligence units. If the foreign policy president in 1984 is to be essentially different in power than during the seventies, his rivals will have to be more powerful and more persistent than they have been in the past. Otherwise the president will still be dominant by default. The only restraints that really matter are those enforced by competition from actual people.

The Rivals—The Public, Interest Groups, and the Senate

> Although presidents have rivals for power in foreign affairs, the rivals do not usually succeed. Presidents prevail not only because they may have superior resources but because their potential opponents are weak, divided, or believe they should not control foreign policy.[10]

The general public is ignorant of most questions; ignorance is a form of weakness. This weakness favors the president since it debilitates his competitors. Polls of the future are likely to express support for the president during international crises, just as in the past during the Bay of Pigs, the bombing of Haiphong, and so on.

The reasons for this initial public support are varied and include: general ignorance, faith in the president, and absence of cue-giving interest groups. The general public is usually indifferent and always incompetent to act as a rival to the president in foreign affairs. In domestic politics, most important questions have a long history—medicare, civil rights, etc.—opinions are more highly developed, interest groups tend

---

[10] Wildavsky, *op. cit.,* p. 95.

to be more numerous, and costs and benefits are more tangible to citizens. The general public is an important element in political calculations in domestic affairs; in foreign initiatives they are an initial presidential resource.

Initial public support for little understood presidential actions is unlikely to change. Approval in public opinion polls for the Nixon China visit and his new economic policies reflect a combination of public indifference, elite approval, ignorance, and faith in the president. Popular opinion constitutes a constraint only when it is organized into attentive issue-publics that can understand and interpret presidential action and pass this information on to less attentive publics. Due to the Indochina experience, a small, attentive, and informed issue-public has formed. It functions a little like the China lobby of the forties and fifties. The president may develop rivals from another segment of the public—the emergence of ethnic nationalism may have an effect on selected foreign policy areas, such as the Middle East.

The Vietnam Issue—Public

In 1964 only a handful of individuals had any opinions or information about Vietnam. By 1968, a highly developed, though small, issue-public had grown up around the war. This public exists at a number of levels: student groups, academic experts, journalists, and politicians. The length of the war and availability of analysis have produced a public that scrutinizes every presidential move very closely. They point out perceived inconsistencies as well' as spread and interpret information—in the process reducing the information costs to other participants. One of the most important powers that a president has is the power to persuade; he often takes on the guise of the "village explainer" who interprets complex events for our understanding. The president no longer has a monopoly of information on Vietnam, and this limits his persuasive powers. For instance, careful probing by journalists during Cambodia and Laos undermined administration claims of victory. Politicians in Congress pointed out breaches of faith between what the administration promised and delivered—the critics' remarks in turn were amplified throughout the country. The collective impact of this public may have undermined public faith in the credibility of the president. The general public may be supportive of initial presidential actions, but the issue-public may corrode that confidence in the aftermath. In complicated political decisions, there are always inconsistencies and half-truths; the difference is that in Vietnam decisions more people have been watching more closely and telling others about these failings. This clearly constitutes a check on the presidential monopoly in foreign affairs because it escalates the costs of error.

As for the future of this Vietnam issue-public, several things remain unclear for 1984. To some extent, expertise and experience in watching Vietnam are not transferable to other foreign policy questions; this means that as importance shifts to other foreign policy areas, some elements of this public are no longer operational.

There are some generally applicable elements of the Vietnam lessons. Opposition to and careful analysis of presidential actions improve with practice. Given the real experience in paying the costs of an unproductive foreign war, there is going to be some natural reticence to incurring them in the future. JFK's words "pay any price, bear any burden" ring differently today than when they were initially spoken. The analogy of Vietnam, like the analogy of Munich before it, will be frequently cited with effect. Now, there are simply a lot of people around who recall the elements of the story, and who are able to repeat the causal connections with practiced ease. The past parable of appeasement strengthening totalitarian dictatorships is giving way to a more contemporary story complete with storytellers.

Ethnic Nationalism

Another attentive foreign policy public may be growing, one not directly related to Vietnam. Remembering that public indifference, or ignorance, is a presidential asset in foreign policy, the growth of attentive publics serves as a constraint on executive action. There may be a number of publics for specific issues, growing as a by-product of ethnic nationalism. Ethnic groupings have always been the source of some activity on foreign policy questions—for instance, isolationist sympathies among those of German and Italian descent prior to World War II. Another more recent example is the influence of American Jews on policy toward Israel. Many black groups have developed foreign policy attitudes toward African nations, particularly Rhodesia and South Africa, and to a lesser extent toward the Middle East. Ethnic nationalism among other groups seems to be on the rise; Polish and Italian political associations are forming in the industrial Northeast, and Chicano groups in California. This trend could spread to many other groupings. It is conceivable that this recent wave of ethnic sentiment will produce a number of publics attentive to foreign policy issues concerning national homelands or ethnic identities. The most recent example involving a sense of ethnic identity is the "foreign policy" of the Jewish Defense League toward the U.S.S.R. over Soviet Jewry.

Many of these emerging ethnic publics have substantial numbers of voters—that is a pretty good beginning to influence foreign policy. Since such groups frequently live in ethnic neighborhoods, they tend to be represented in political institutions. Thus there are direct links between groups and elected officials that tend to amplify their influence. As group consciousness increases and possibly spreads into foreign policy concerns, there are ready-made paths for political expression.

Ethnic nationalism is not necessarily going to directly detract from presidential power in foreign affairs. At the present time only a very few ethnic groups have a "foreign policy," although many ethnics are attentive to events concerning national homelands. And it is conceivable that such groups may constitute a presidential resource on some questions, such as the sale of jets to Israel. But ethnic sentiments are not a resource which is under the total control of the president as are his military and informational powers, and their use requires adjustments on his part. A president's attempts to use domestic political groups to further his preferences sometimes lead to difficulties. His choices may be perceived by such publics as American Jews or Arabs as either not doing enough or doing too much for Israel.

Linkages

Are there connections between the foreign policy issue-publics, arising out of Vietnam or ethnic nationalism, and Congress? Such a link would increase the willingness of many legislators to challenge the president. For ethnic groupings the answer has already been discussed. Those groups with sufficient numbers, concentrated populations, and some level of organization already have congressional voices. The obvious example is the New York City congressional delegation and their position on Israel. Electoral links are the bonds that best insure group representation. Because of their smaller constituencies and frequent election, members of the House of Representatives may be more susceptible to ethnic group influence—although senators are by no means immune. Senators, on the other hand, may be more receptive to the national issue-publics of the type generated by the war. Such a public provides some senators with a receptive audience for their views, supportive information, and monetary help. Senator McCarthy's 1968 campaign was financed and staffed largely out of this public. Both kinds of publics provide elected representatives with some support and, in some cases, with a motive for opposing or supporting a particular presidential foreign policy goal. Since the source of such activity is independent of presidential preferences, the executive branch has a new potential source of competition.

Congressional Rivals—The Senate

The House and Senate are potentially the most effective rivals to the president in foreign affairs. They have always had an impressive array of instruments, frequently used in domestic politics but still as yet rarely employed in foreign affairs: power of the purse, including the ability to attach conditions to appropriations; investigative committees and hearings to publicize conflicts; as well as the ability to confirm presidential appointments and to grant or withhold support for the administration in other areas of legislation. The effect of these powers, as Senator Church said, "amounts to so much idle talk, unless a majority proves willing to invoke it."[11]

The fact that occasional controversies have erupted between the Congress and presidency in defense appropriations points out that the powers of the legislature are substantial when exercised. Typically, internal rivalries within the executive branch have formed the cleavages through which congressmen sometimes can enter into the determination of defense and

---

[11] Quoted in Dvorin, *op cit.,* p. 10.

foreign policy.[12] Whether such rivalries are between the armed forces or the Secretary of Defense, disputes among experts stimulate the activities of lay political leaders. Other sources of division also exist, for instance differences between the Departments of Defense and State on Israel. There are also disputes involving the Central Intelligence Agency. The frequency and visibility of executive branch disputes may have been reduced in recent years by the practice of concentrating many important decision-making powers within the White House itself. Disputes within the presidential staff usually do not become as public as those between the services and cabinet departments. The Nixon decision to visit China surprised the State department as much as Congress. Obviously the occasional opportunities for congressional intervention created by fallings-out among executive agencies do not give representatives a regular or predictable role in the determination of policy. In the future, congressional participation may be more frequent and less dependent on executive schisms.

The shape of Senate-presidential relations for 1984 may have been drastically altered by the watershed period between the Johnson presidency and the invasion of Cambodia. These years were marked by the full exercise of the president's war-creating powers. They culminated in the invasion of Cambodia, *which was justified by the president entirely on his constitutional powers of commander in chief and enforced by the real power of decision.* The Cambodian invasion produced the Cooper-Church amendment, basically a written version of what the president was promising to do.

The desire for some collective institutional assertion by the Senate of its foreign policy role had been building up for some time. Some senators were getting tired of the two presidencies. During the Cambodian debate, Senator Fulbright quoted an earlier Foreign Relations Committee report:

> Our country has come far toward the concentration in its national executive of unchecked power over foreign relations, particularly over the disposition and use of the armed forces.

[12] Louis Anthony Dexter, "Congressmen and the Making of Military Policy," in Robert L. Peabody and Nelson W. Polsby (eds.), *New Perspectives on the House of Representatives*, 2d ed. (Chicago: Rand McNally, 1969), pp. 175–195.

So far has this process advanced that, in the committee's view, it is no longer accurate to characterize our government, in matters of foreign relations, as one of separated powers checked and balanced against each other.[13]

Fulbright continued in his own speech to state:

The notion that the authority to commit the United States to war is an executive prerogative, or even a divided or uncertain one, is one which has grown up only in recent decades. It is the result primarily of a series of emergencies or alleged emergencies which have enhanced executive power, fostered attitudes of urgency and anxiety, and given rise to a general disregard for constitutional procedure.[14]

As this debate progressed, many of the Cooper-Church's proponents expressed suspicion of the information provided by the executive and the military. The implications of this debate are clear: a number of senators are unhappy with the president's total control over foreign affairs and are unconvinced of the good will or competence of the executive department. The lessons described earlier have attracted strong subscribers. The president's resources of knowledge and competence clearly count for less than they did. Are these sentiments idiosyncratic to Vietnam? Or is senatorial assertiveness linked to more permanent political, institutional, and systemic roots?

It might very well be that the full blossoming of the power of the foreign policy president contained some of the elements of senatorial opposition. Presidential control over foreign affairs appears to have grown tighter since Eisenhower, who consulted a bipartisan group of senators including LBJ about his Indochina decisions. In recent years, such outside consultation has become rarer—Cambodia was a surprise to friends as well as foes of the administration. Prior to the Vietnam war, senators interested in foreign or defense policy had exerted whatever influence they had by lobbying at the White House. Professor Wildavsky cites the examples of Senators Jackson and Vandenberg, who lobbied for their views on the Polaris and the Marshall Plan, respectively. Senator Fulbright himself has tried to influence presidents from

[13] Quoted in Dvorin, *op. cit.*, p. 7.
[14] *Ibid.*

Roosevelt to Nixon through direct personal diplomacy. However, since the president's power has become so substantial over foreign affairs, there has been little need to include dissonant advisors in discussions about policy. They were simply not needed to effect the preferred policy. One of the consequences of total control is that the president can exclude whom he desires—thus exit Fulbright and Under-Secretary George Ball. With the closing of the opportunity to effectively lobby the White House, many senators are expending those energies in public and through the institutional framework provided by the Senate. Much of the effort behind the Cooper-Church amendment might have been expended differently in the past. Once senatorial action, through committee or floor action, becomes the means of influence—as private lobbying had been in the past—then it is the "beaten path" which in politics is often preferred.

There is some evidence to indicate that the newly beaten path has attracted a number of senatorial travelers. Within a short time period, a number of actions were recently attempted and threatened. The Senate Foreign Relations Committee said it would cut off funds for military aid programs unless the executive produced a Pentagon document. Meanwhile, a judiciary subcommittee began hearings on legislation that would compel governmental officials to appear before congressional committees unless the president specifically evoked executive privilege. Other demands were voiced to give congressmen access to CIA information. Senator Javits introduced a measure that would limit the president's ability to undertake emergency military action to no more than a month without explicit congressional approval. And of course the demand for a "date certain" for withdrawal was repeated. Senator Hugh Scott, the Republican leader, joined in the drive for curbing the president's war powers and said: "The time has come, when Congress will not be denied the right to participate, in accordance with the Constitution, in the whole enormous business of how wars are begun."[15] Of course, all these threats are not going to necessarily come to pass, and even if they do, there is no guarantee that congressional participation necessarily changes policy outcomes. However, the

[15] John W. Finney, "Congress: For the President Some Ties That Bind," *The New York Times,* August 1, 1971.

passivity of the Senate in foreign policy is clearly at an end. The president has a rival for control where previously he had none.

The availability and temporary popularity of senatorial modes of action are not enough to guarantee influence beyond the Indochina war. There has to be some more lasting motivation that keeps senators participating; otherwise the balance between the Senate and the presidency is liable to lapse into a modified pre-Vietnam arrangement. After all, the president's powers have remained essentially the same; only the willingness of his rivals to abdicate responsibility is changing. One way to gauge the effect of recent experience, for 1984, is to locate possible carry-overs into the future. We already know something of the general lessons of the war; now the question becomes who has been taught?

The Vietnam Experience as Senatorial Education

In the short run, the antiwar senators are gaining experience in opposing the president on foreign policy. Efforts to restrict the president, like a lot of other things, improve with practice. More judgment and discernment are used in picking fights. The ineffectiveness of general resolutions has given way to more specific and potentially more effective limitations: draft ceilings, specific dates for withdrawal, etc. Many senators now have a better idea of the range of presidential evasion of restrictions, and can plan more effectively for such contingencies. This kind of experience is transitive to other foreign policy issue areas and raises the collective capacity of the Senate to compete with the president.

A less tangible, but potentially important by-product of the Vietnam experience has been its impact on the attitudes of senators toward future foreign involvement. Although the final roll call on the Cooper-Church amendment, 75 to 20, is not the best indicator of senatorial assertiveness in foreign affairs, its purpose was clearly to restrict the president in Cambodia. Taking this vote as a benchmark, in 1984, nine of the co-sponsors of the amendment will be sixty-five years old or younger. Of the twenty-eight senators who will be under sixty-five by the time of the 99th Congress, twenty-four voted for the final measure. The safety of incumbency will keep many of these senators serving well into the eighties. This group includes the most vocal critics of international military involvement: McGovern, Kennedy, Church, Hughes, Eagleton, and many others. One way to perpetuate a lesson of foreign policy failure is to tie it to the continuity in office of those who underwent that educational experience.

Continuing Difficulties

Even with this increased competition from the Senate in foreign affairs, the president still enjoys the advantages discussed earlier. His powers are not as awesome as they were in the sixties, but they are still substantial. Presidents still have a considerable bargaining advantage over the Senate. Because of the nature of presidential precedents, which form the effective base for future exercise of executive power, the president can argue persuasively that any present restriction is a potentially dangerous future restriction, given the emergency nature of foreign affairs. President Nixon finds himself in a position, described by Thomas Schelling, of intersecting negotiations.[16] In such a situation, the advantage is with the party that can point out he has the most to lose—he is most committed to his bargaining position, because a loss means loss in necessary future power. Presidential partisans make this argument, which usually finds resonance even among critics. For a variety of reasons, factual and mythical, the notion that foreign policy decisions require speed and decisiveness seems to be inherent in this area.[17] This redounds to the benefit of the president.

Still another problem with senatorial involvement in directing foreign affairs is their sporadic, or narrowly specific, interest in this area. The executive department is in daily control of decisions—this tends to undermine legislative power as effectively as Michel's Iron Law of Oligarchy forecloses member control over leaders in organizations.

Despite these and other obvious difficulties of the Senate acting as a persistent and effective rival to the president, a

---

[16] Thomas G. Schelling, *The Strategy of Conflict* (New York: Oxford University Press, 1968), p. 30.
[17] Examples of nations who make war decisions by committee are Israel and North Vietnam.

trend is emerging toward a more active role. Presidents have become more appreciative of the costs of not considering the Senate in foreign policy actions—the House can still be taken for granted. These costs take numerous forms: intense investigation and publicizing of administration errors, defeats in other areas like the SST, reversals on court nominees, or the 1971 Senate decision to block the administration's foreign-aid bill. In part many of these defeats are attributable to the "practiced" opposition coalition that has evolved partially out of foreign policy fights.

Circumstances of Institutional Change

The most dramatic shift in congressional-presidential relations between the present and 1984 will be in their relative power over the conduct of foreign relations. The pre-Vietnam presidency will have given way to a situation in which the Senate has a larger—though far from dominant—role. The climate of opinion that supported past presidential hegemony is now changing. The consensus on national interest and the attendant faith in the completeness and effectiveness of presidential prosecution has been severely undermined. There is a developing social and political base for expression of this disenchantment and other concerns through the development of foreign policy issue-publics based on antiwar sentiments and ethnic nationalism. These publics have links with elected representatives in Congress. Congress itself, particularly the Senate, has been increasingly active in asserting its own powers. The energies of individual senators, interested in foreign affairs, who had been previously used to lobby the White House, are now finding increased expression in the Senate itself. Furthermore, senators have received an education in tactics—and conceptions of their role in foreign affairs are changing—as a result of the Vietnam war. These formative experiences will be carried into the eighties by the continuity in office of those educated. The experience of Indochina, like that of Munich before it, is finding the public and institutional basis necessary to act as a constraint on presidential action.

One of the reasons this essay has lingered so long on the relative power and effectiveness of the Senate and presidency in foreign affairs is that this is the area which was most likely to change. The reason is simple; it was the area of institutional relations that was characterized by the most unexercised power on the part of a participant—Congress. Since the failure of president's rivals constituted a large element of his own control, increased competition could have the largest effect on diminishing executive powers. In other words, the past reticence of the Senate to act as a rival provided the most latitude for a shift of relative institutional powers.

By contrast, the next section on the House of Representatives illustrates the capacity of an institution to dampen the effects of short-term changes, and 1984 is not very far away. In understanding the future of institutions, sources of resistance to change are as important as the specification of the conditions of change.

The House of Representatives

Of all the institutions of national government the House is least likely to change substantially by 1984. It is insulated from presidential influence by the seniority system, from shifts in national opinion by safe constituencies, and even from elements of its own membership by strict division of labor. The president and Senate have been discussed in terms of their effects on one another and the effect of the public on both. But changes of significance in the House are changes that affect its structure and internal disposition of power. The most impressive elements of the House are its narrowly specialized senior members, set in a rigid committee system, processing vast amounts of diverse, complicated legislation in great detail.[18] Costs of this performance, unrivaled by most other legislative bodies, are slowness and frequently conservatism.

What are the stable "facts" of congressional committee system that will be working their influence on the 99th Congress in 1984? Barring any major change in seniority, those who will chair the great standing committees in 1984 are already tenured members of the House. In some instances, they may

---

[18] Nelson W. Polsby, "The Institutionalization of the U.S. House of Representatives," *American Political Science Review* 62 (March 1968), 114–168. See also Polsby, *Congress and the Presidency,* 2d ed. (Englewood Cliffs, N.J.: Prentice Hall, 1971).

already be committee chairmen—the remarkable Wilbur Mills
could conceivably still be head of Ways and Means at age
seventy-three. Congressional leadership seems to be congenial to long life. There are several conceivable circumstances under which changes could occur in the disposition
of chairmanships: A modification of seniority rule; the defeat
of some senior members due to increased local competition;
sharp changes in the composition of the House; or a combination of all of these things.

Seniority

The seniority system is perhaps the single most visible issue
of institutional reform. To this system of selecting chairmen
are attributed the collective evils of congressional intransigence and conservatism. The implication of many critical
arguments is that a reform in seniority would release a flood
of liberal legislation now bottled up in strong committees.
There is little doubt that some modification of the system
would be healthy. But there is little evidence to indicate that
the House would suddenly become a liberal legislation machine. The most effective chairmen are those who avoid
antagonizing the occasional majorities that form on important
issues; if there is an intense majority for an issue like
medicare, the relevant chairman cannot block it for long. The
House, like all legislative bodies, has very few and only occasional majorities; instead it is composed of members of
varying commitments, constituencies, and of groups with varying political and ideological cohesion. It is the absence of
liberal majorities that makes possible the frequent success of
some conservative committee chairmen. The industrious minority of Southern Democratic committee chairmen have had
the advantage over the sometimes less industrious and as-
suredly strategically placed liberal minority. Furthermore the
success of conservatives can also be attributed to their more
modest goals of blocking rather than passing legislation. The
House has decentralized power into many functioning committees. The greater the degree of decentralization, the more
opportunities for blockage.

The success of some conservative chairmen is attributable
to the failure of their opponents to mobilize a liberal majority,
the parliamentary and political skill of some senior members,

and to their strategic placement due to tenure. In the past, Southern legislators frequently came from relatively safe constituencies. Where the Democratic party predominated, they came in at an early age and due to their electoral safety and career choices they stayed a long time. Naturally, they developed an advantage in accumulated service. Northern Democrats tended to arrive later in life, represent more competitive districts, and more frequently left the House for other careers.[19] This situation seems to be changing: There are more Northern safe seats, Southern congressional elections are becoming more competitive, and some liberal issue-oriented Democrats are seriously pursuing the House as a long-term career. The effects of these kinds of shifts take time to materialize. However, once effected they endure.

Naturally the system of seniority is looking better to some liberal Democratic congressmen who are increasingly becoming its beneficiaries. They do not wholeheartedly embrace all the system's features, but they realize that their viewpoints are frequently minority views—in the House and nation—and as such would gain some marginal advantage under seniority.[20] On the whole, these legislators and others do not favor the system's total elimination. Most House members are pleased with some aspects of seniority, many enjoy substantial, though narrow, power through committee and subcommittee chairmanships, most appreciate the competence and knowledge encouraged by incentives to long-term service on specific committees, and many see the system as promising future power to themselves.

There will probably be some modification in the House practice of seniority rule. All that would be required to effect such a change would be a decision on the part of the majority

---

[19] Raymond Wolfinger and Joan Hollinger, "Safe Seats, Seniority, and Power in Congress," in Peabody and Polsby (eds.), *op. cit.*, pp. 55–77.

[20] Insofar as there exists anything that can be called a majority in the nation, that majority is the voting majority who are "unyoung, unpoor, unblack"—Richard Scammon and Ben Wattenberg, *The Real Majority* (New York: Coward-McCann, 1970). Once beyond these demographic characteristics, there are few majorities in legislative politics. Instead, coalitions of minorities form the occasional legislative majorities necessary for victory. Sheer numbers, intensity of opinion, level of organization, and strategic placement of minority viewpoints determine which minorities have the largest say in legislative outcomes.

caucus to abandon seniority as the sole criterion in the selection of chairmen. Many elements of the press have been editorializing for such a change, some political activists have used the system as a symbol of intransigence in Congress. And there are constant efforts by some House members to change the process—a group of these reformers even won a small victory in 1971. A great deal of promise has been attached to the elimination of seniority: that it would create a liberal-progressive Congress, by eliminating the stifling rule of Southern chairmen. If the rule is modified, this promise will not be completely fulfilled. A number of proposals for reform contain some elements of the old system, such as election among the senior members, and these are most likely to pass. Talented conservatives, like Wilbur Mills, are likely to get elected chairmen on their expertise and skill. Remember the problem with this system is *not* senility and incompetence —rather the combination of experience, skill, knowledge, and conservatism. The House majority is not particularly liberal. In 1971, when liberals in the Democratic caucus tried to oust a conservative chairman from the head of an unimportant committee, they were soundly defeated. Seniority has been a consideration in committee assignments and chairmanships at least since the Civil War, and because of the House's need for the specialized knowledge of experienced members, it will continue to be important even after rules changes. The effect of such changes will be to deselect some incompetent chairmen, but that does not mean liberals will replace them. A slightly modified seniority rule would simply mean selection among a larger number of oldsters, open election means competition for the votes of a possibly conservative majority.

Defeat of Senior Members

The defeat of some senior members would undoubtedly affect the disposition of chairmanships in 1984. The hope is that increased competition, by Southern blacks or new eighteen-year-old voters, will turn once safe districts into competitive areas. Several things militate against this change. First, senior Southern congressmen and others in urban Northern states often have close ties with state legislators, who draw district lines. Even with the "one man, one vote" rule there is substantial room for art in drawing districts with necessary majorities. Outspoken liberals sometimes lack the same friendly home ties with local politicians. Al Lowenstein's defeat was insured by redistricting in New York; a similar fate has befallen Bella Abzug, and may face William Clay. Second, the elimination of a senior member does not necessarily mean immediate improvement. This sad fact was proved in 1970 when Father Drinan, after a vigorous campaign, defeated Phillip Philbin, second-ranking member of the Armed Forces Committee; later, chairman Mendel Rivers died, and equally conservative F. Edward Hébert became chairman. There are a lot of conservative senior members to go through before substantial change can occur. Third, there is little indication that a wholesale dumping of incumbents can occur—in 1968 only six were beaten in the general election, and fewer than that in 1970.

A number of recent newspaper articles and statements by political activists have argued that the 25 million newly enfranchised eighteen to twenty-four year-olds may affect the reelection chances of conservative committee chairmen. Districts such as those of William Colmer of Rules, Richard Ichord of the House Internal Security Committee, and Harley Staggers of Commerce have new voters greater in number than the size of past election margins.[21] The argument is that the new voters may swing elections in such districts. The effect probably will not be as great as the promise for a number of reasons. Scammon and Wattenberg, and others, have pointed out that the new young voters will be a minority, diffused geographically, with a low probability of voting, and most importantly, they are divided among themselves.[22] In many Southern districts, George Wallace enjoys considerable support among the current and future young voters. The preponderance of working young over student young—despite differential voting turnout—may effectively cancel out the effect of these new voters by interjecting new groups of adversaries. There will be an effect in districts with large universities, where numerous students augment liberal voting

[21] Warren Weaver, Jr., "Young Voters May Change the Make-up of Congress in '72," *The New York Times,* September 20, 1971.
[22] One such argument is found in "How Will Youth Vote?" *Newsweek,* October 25, 1971, pp. 28–49. See also Scammon and Wattenberg, *op. cit.,* Part 2.

residents. Such districts are not numerous. Whatever their effect on presidential elections, the young will probably not figure as an anti-chairman bloc of votes.

Short-Term Changes in the Composition of Congress

This third possibility is the best—sharp changes in the composition of Congress. There have been three great legislative pushes in the twentieth century. The first was under Woodrow Wilson, who effectively used the House Democratic caucus—in the absence of the modern seniority system—to enforce his will on Congress. For a variety of reasons that state of affairs is unlikely to return. The other two periods of legislative success were the New Deal and the Great Society. Both were made possible by lopsided congressional majorities—resulting from the depression and the nomination of Barry Goldwater. Even though chairmen did not change, the heavy House majorities made it possible to get legislation through. Such an event usually requires an economic or political catastrophe. Perhaps the most important example of the influence of short-term changes is Chairman Wilbur Mills, who switched his position on Medicare when he discovered the votes were against him; in switching his position, he swung around and assumed a leadership position in passing this legislation.[23] Lopsided congressional majorities are the products of heavy presidential election victories. Since the electorate that brings in this new Congress tends to be temporarily swollen by a "surge" of occasional voters, the return to normal partisan patterns usually means that such majorities are frequently temporary.

The House Black Caucus

The fourth source of internal House change might be the increased participation of blacks in congressional politics. By the eighties one observer says that the congressional black caucus will have grown to thirty members. There are several

[23] John Manley, "Wilbur D. Mills: A Study in Congressional Influence," *American Political Science Review* 63 (June 1969), 442–464. Theodore Marmor, "The Congress: Medicare Politics and Policy," Sindler (ed.), *op. cit.,* pp. 2–67.

reasons that work for enhancing the importance of blacks in the House: increased political competition in the South due to black implementation of the Voting Rights Act of 1965; population shifts creating central city "safe" districts for blacks; and increased political participation by black voters. The collective impact of these changes will be exerting some effect in 1984, but several factors may keep this impact from being as dramatic as many hope. First, even with perfect representation of black voters, they remain a minority—11 percent of the population figures out to a little under forty-eight congressional seats; even with black congressmen representing some white districts that number will probably not exceed forty-eight. The tenure requirements of the seniority system dampen the effect of even safe urban seats—Adam Clayton Powell represented his Harlem district for a decade and a half before becoming Chairman of Education and Labor. Furthermore, the competition for leadership in black politics, like any other emerging politics, is keen and time-consuming. The precariousness of leadership increases turnover, and thus reduces seniority, as in the case of Powell. Also, congressional careers have to compete with other attractive political offices, especially as more city halls open up; this again reduces black seniority.

Still another factor that has to be reckoned with is the diversity within the black caucus—machine Democrats, liberals, and a few radicals, all possessing different views of political action. There is also the problem of white-controlled state legislatures, which may gerrymander black seats out of existence from time to time. Also many of the radical white and black congressmen are dependent upon a mass movement for reelection, and it is difficult to maintain that kind of momentum over a decade.

Black politicians face an additional problem unique to leaders whose constituencies have high expectations of political action. In the words of one prominent California state legislator: "To my constituents, representation means that they can see their legislator—I have to spend a lot of time in my district to guard myself against charges of remoteness and insensitivity." This legislator and others in a similar situation consciously spend less time on legislative business in order to make frequent and visible appearances at home. The dilemma for black congressmen is that influence in the House typically means knowledge about specialized areas of legislative business; that kind of knowledge is synonymous with constant, hard attention to low-publicity business—but his maintenance in office depends on constituents unsympathetic to the remoteness and invisibility of such a role.

Some black representatives have responded to the foreclosing of immediate access to House power and the demands of their constituents for visible representation by carving out a role for themselves as skillful publicists for the cities. Shirley Chisholm and others have made this response. They have proved exceptions to the general conception of House office as a low-publicity job. Their effectiveness will not lie in the exercise of institutional power, but rather in their ability to gain public support for the plight of their constituents.

Black influence within Congress may be felt in other ways. It is unlikely that radical black representatives could win committee chairmanships under open caucus elections, and under a seniority system all black representatives will suffer the liabilities already discussed (except perhaps black machine politicians). Still, blacks are a sizeable block of votes, united by a common condition of their supporters if not their own views. At least through 1984, the influence of blacks will be that of an internal House pressure group rather than as committee chairmen. As an interest group they have several advantages: a sizeable block of votes for some issues, access to liberal allies due to ideological ties, influence in the selection of Democratic presidential nominees, and—perhaps most important—a high level of talent. Like the Irish and others many of the best have gone into politics.

Change and Institutional Stability

Perhaps the most visible and important internal political development of the past decade has been the increased power of blacks. The ability of the House of Representatives to blunt the effects of such a major change on their own distribution of internal power illustrates the genuine toughness of its institutional skin. This insulation protects the strict internal division of labor that makes it possible to process complex legislation by parceling it out to highly specialized committees. Seniority rewards House service; long-time service in turn facilitates specialization. Since the House's effectiveness against the Senate and president depend on this system, it is only natural that insulation has developed to protect against outside changes. Whatever the virtues of such a system, it is apparent that the cumulative effect of institutional insulation, in the case of the House, severely dampens the effect of outside change. When making predictions about the future of such an institution, it is always more accurate to err on the side of inertia.

Normally, when one looks to predict the future, the natural tendency is to look to the world and say that changes in the political environment cause changes in political institutions. To some extent stable institutions create their own environment—the House is simply a highly developed example. The earlier section on the relations between the Senate and the president in foreign affairs sought to locate a means by which changes in the environment could find institutional expression. The effects of those changes were possible due to the existence of hitherto unexercised potential on the part of the Senate—changes had a means of institutional expression. The second example, the House of Representatives, demonstrates the ability of an institution to dampen change, to perpetuate its present form into the near future. Although the House will probably be successful in maintaining its internal distribution of power, some of its members may carve out outside roles— such as black urban spokesmen. Outside changes in this case are not reflected in visible institutional change, but rather in new forms of political expression that use the institution as a base rather than as an instrument. In foreign policy the growth of ethnic nationalism could spur some House members into a spokesman role in behalf of their constituents—again using their position as a base.

The previous sections have dealt with the potential for change in the shape of institutional form. The Senate will be more competitive with the president in the conduct of foreign affairs, and the House will change little. The final section makes some conjectures about changes in the modes taken by political controversies. Given what is known about institutional inclinations, how will they react to changes in the form of political conflict?

Future Issues of Importance

The names of the issues propelling the politics of 1984 are already pretty well known. Fundamental questions typically take a long time to resolve in American politics. The slavery question, which divided the Constitutional Convention in 1787, continued to split the nation until the Civil War. The question of equality remains in America as elsewhere. Even relatively minor changes require decades—the expansion of medical insurance to the elderly has a thirty-year history stretching from the New Deal to the Great Society.[24] Since major problems characteristically take a long time to be resolved, the agenda of 1984 will undoubtedly include: race, poverty, environment, health care, and maybe even foreign war. Since the issues themselves will not dramatically change, the interesting question for future politics is: Will institutional political actors pursue their goals differently than in the past?

Politics and Scarcity

Although politics has always involved winners and losers, political actors have not always acted upon that assumption. Many historians have pointed out the fact that the characteristic view of earlier American politicians was that this is a land of plenty. As a result, conflicts were not always direct; instead relations among actors were predicated on the notion that mutual benefit was derived from cooperation among those who petitioned for governmental services. This perspective changes with a realization of scarcity. The problem of political action has been redefined. For liberals it is no longer simply a matter of passing social legislation, but also of curbing less desirable governmental commitments to free money for the alleviation of poverty—or whatever goal is selected from the list.

Perhaps the modal words of the presidential campaigns of 1968 were: "a gross misallocation of national priorities." Behind this and other similar phrases was the notion that the politically deliverable goods were scarce, not plentiful. There was a finite limit to money, to national will, and other such

[24] Marmor, in Sindler (ed.), *op. cit.*

things. Many arguments against the Vietnam war were couched in terms of wasted resources, passed up alternative uses for the money; contrasts were drawn between amounts spent for munitions and amounts spent for housing, health, or other social programs. Reinforcing this sense of scarcity and waste were trends in other political issues. The environmentalists emphasized the depletion of national resources like fossil fuels, and the general costs of productivity. The dollar crisis, the balance of payments crisis, and other half-understood economic crises pushed for a realization that the period of American economic hegemony was nearing an end. In local and state politics so-called taxpayer revolts also gained widespread publicity. The cumulative effect of these arguments has been to emphasize the long-known fact that the benefits of politics are limited—someone gains and someone loses.

A recent example of this sense of scarcity in action has been the opposition of radicals on the Berkeley City Council to the size of the police budget. They reasoned that money spent for police was money denied to the creation of childcare centers. On a national level, the same reasoning went into some senatorial opposition to the anti-ballistic missile. The way to facilitate social programs under conditions of scarcity is to minimize expenditures for other uses. The once dreary area of budgeting is becoming a visible center of political controversy.

The notion that political goods are scarce has encouraged the growth of two related political forms. First, there is an increase in what could be classed as a consumer-oriented mode of political action—attempts to increase the value received from expenditures. Efficiency of expenditures frees money for other purposes. And second, actual opposition to expenditures for disliked purposes. Congress will provide a receptive arena for both forms of political action.

In the past the most outspoken legislative voices for curbing expenses and increased efficiency had been conservatives. This is now changing. Economy, efficiency, and budget cutting are increasingly the instruments of those concerned with expanding social programs. The most successful practitioner of consumer-oriented politics is Ralph Nader; his closest analogue in Congress is Senator William Proxmire. In form many of their arguments are similar. The targets for close scrutiny are disliked by the investigator—General Motors or defense contractors. Success of the endeavor depends upon its effect on the public—and thus requires vast amounts of publicity. The reasons why Congress is particularly receptive to this form of political action give us a clue to increased congressional activity in the next decade.

The aspirations of legislators and the instruments of Congress are congenial to consumer investigation for several reasons. First, many senators want to be president, which entails carving out a national constituency by whatever instruments are available. Ambition is quite a reliable source of political energy. Second, a useful engine lies in a congressional investigation. When such an investigation is launched into a specification of waste, it yields a vast amount of publicity and notoriety as well as creating an appreciative national constituency. The publicity is necessary for the task, and the notoriety is helpful in recruiting investigators. Third, the existing norms of both houses encourage the goal of efficiency. Fourth, there are new investigators. Such investigations in the past were usually avoided by liberals who had other goals—but those goals are now tied directly to the diminution of other expenses. Hence the scope of congressional waste-hunts expands because the number and goals of the hunters themselves increase. Already underway are investigations into the shortcomings of organized medicine, auto manufacturers, and defense contractors; the list will grow as time progresses.

The other form of congressional response to the politics of scarcity is the actual opposition to vast and expensive programs. Recent conflicts include the ABM, the SST, and the Mansfield European troop reduction plan. Once again, Congress has always checked the president on domestic governmental spending—but there has been a widening of targets. Social legislation is no longer the only target for serious and organized opposition. Expensive defense commitments now face such opposition. Denying the purse is rapidly becoming a major tactic of liberals as well as conservatives.

An example of an available senatorial instrument turned to new purposes is the filibuster. Previously it had been used almost exclusively to kill civil rights legislation. Since it was goring the liberal ox, the filibuster was damned by many. It looks better these days; thus far it has been used as a tactic by those opposed to the supersonic transport, loan guarantees for failing big businesses, and extensions of the draft. Senator

Alan Cranston has said he could no longer support moves to limit debate:

> When our dislike for filibusters becomes more important to us than our distrust of the draft or our revulsion with Vietnam, then we ought to take another look at the filibuster and its legitimate use.[25]

Senate liberals are availing themselves of an instrument useful to intense and relatively numerous minorities. As denying the purse becomes an important and constructive goal to liberals, a number of useful instruments will be rediscovered.

As the filibuster example illustrates, Congress already possesses instruments and opportunities to stop action. With shifting definitions and goals of political action, these instruments are finding new targets. Another illustration of increased liberal use of existing institutional characteristics is the 1971 decision to temporarily kill the administration's foreign-aid bill. Senate liberals who objected to aid for Cambodia and military aid for other nations joined another intense minority of conservatives who opposed the whole notion of foreign aid, to jointly vote down the aid bill. The relative ease with which coalitions of diverse minorities can form majorities to kill legislation in Congress has long been an institutional characteristic. The leverage that intense minorities enjoy in such a system is finding new expressions. In this example, the Senate liberals will gain important concessions from the administration before any aid proposal passes.

Just as the past reticence of the Senate to assert itself in foreign affairs left room for present institutional expansion of their role, the past reticence of liberals to mount serious opposition to some spending programs left a similar unexercised potential. This is now changing.

The politics of scarcity dovetails with the increased congressional role in defense and foreign policy. Most of the targets of economy-minded liberals are going to be related to defense because it is expensive and an ideologically acceptable butt. In the past, congressmen have been more interested in domestic politics than in foreign and defense policy. This was the case because the political payoffs for legislators were

[25] Alan Cranston, "The Congress—The Filibuster: Times Are Changing," *National Journal,* October 9, 1971, p. 2056.

greater when they could provide constituents with tangible benefits—the payoffs in foreign policy were usually invisible to the folks back home. However, as cuts in military expenses are tied directly to increased benefits for constituents, the motivation for many legislators to compete with the president increases. And as already has been noted, they have the wherewithal to compete vigorously.

1984

Presidential hegemony in foreign relations will have been substantially modified by the next decade. The compelling lessons of Vietnam will have replaced the Munich analogy as the dominant metaphor in foreign relations. Although the president's formal powers guarantee him the largest role in the determination of foreign policy, he will face competition from the Senate and segments of the public.

In domestic affairs, the national public debate will be—as usual—between the president and the Senate. Highly visible controversies favor those actors and institutions with the machinery for public debate: notoriety, ambition, access to the press, and so on. In these respects both the Senate and the presidency are amply endowed.

There will be little structural change in the House of Representatives. Although there will be an increasing number of issue-spokesmen arising out of the black caucus, as well as ethnic spokesmen from other groups. Furthermore, both Houses will be the site of frequent, highly visible controversies involving expenditures for social and defense programs.

The increased activity of Congress—in investigating defense expenditures, in publicizing alternative uses for money, and in competing with the president in foreign affairs—should not be confused with a sudden willingness to pass vast amounts of liberal legislation. None of these activities require a concurrent majority of the House and Senate, merely the willingness of some of its members. Major legislative pushes —like the New Deal and Great Society—are the products of extraordinary majorities. Such majorities result from economic and political catastrophes. Predictions about the normal functioning of institutions should not linger on the extraordinary. As must be apparent, such economic and political accidents do happen occasionally and may even occur before 1984.

MICHAEL P. LERNER

was an Assistant Professor of Philosophy at the University of Washington until he was indicted by a federal grand jury for organizing an antiwar demonstration and became part of the "Seattle Conspiracy." He subsequently founded a new national organization of socialists called the New American Movement that is seeking to actualize some of the predictions that he makes in this essay.

the future of
the two-party
system in america

What is the future of the two-party system in America? To answer that question, we must first ask what functions the party system now performs, what interests it serves, and what forces are now at work that may threaten the present conformation of the party system. In this essay, I shall defend an analysis that offers some hope for the development of a new socialist party outside of the framework of the two-party system during the coming dozen years. Briefly, I shall argue that the American party system serves three important systemic purposes:

1. Maintaining the present distribution of wealth and power, making slight adjustments when absolutely necessary.
2. Mediating conflicts of interest among different sections of the capitalist economy.

3. Accommodating pressures from disadvantaged sections of the working population to the extent necessary to stabilize the basic dimensions of the social and economic system.

In its efforts to accommodate working people to the capitalist system, the American party structure has been greatly aided by the successes of American imperialism, which has managed to extract profits from the rest of the world and to use part of those profits to assuage some of the economic demands of American workers. But America's world hegemony has been successfully broken by the combination of the war in Vietnam and the reemergence of serious competition within the capitalist bloc, notably from Japan and the Common Market countries. In the period ahead, monopoly capital will have less room to maneuver, and this will progressively decrease its ability to buy off American workers. As a result, there will be an increase in class consciousness, which will be expressed first through labor agitation, second through existing party mechanisms, and last through the likely emergence of an explicitly socialist party that breaks the political homogeneity of the interparty rivalries and forces the American political arena to deal with questions that have been buried for at least forty years in American life.

I

The presidential elections of the 1960s helped clarify in the public mind why the left has always insisted that the two major parties offer no real choice for those who want change. When all the shouting was over, President Kennedy began to define his New Frontier in ways that were completely congruent with the policies of the 1950s. The development of a war in Vietnam or the delivering of the Telstar system into the hands of AT&T would have made much sense in a Nixon administration, had he won in 1960. The 1964 example is even more dramatic: President Johnson portrayed his Republican opponent as a madman likely to lead the United States into war, only to himself drastically escalate the war in Vietnam. The 1968 election found two defenders of the war facing each other, each promising to end the war gradually if elected. And, if on the crucial issues there was a striking similarity between the two major parties, that similarity was even stronger when one looked more carefully at the interests that both parties served.

Ferdinand Lundberg, author of *America's Sixty Families* and *The Rich and the Super-Rich,* points out that, in fact, we have a one-party system in America with two branches.

> The U.S. can be looked upon as having, in effect, a single party: the Property Party. This party can be looked upon as having two subdivisions: the Republican Party, hostile to accommodating adjustments (hence dubbed "Conservative") and the Democratic Party, of recent decades favoring such adjustments (hence dubbed "Liberal").[1]

In an authoritative study of the Democratic party by G. William Domhoff[2] to be published in 1972, Domhoff shows that the one big party's two branches are financed by the large property holders whom he previously identified in his work on the ruling class, *Who Rules America.*[3] Very often, the same rich men will finance both parties, but even when they do not individually hedge their bets, they can be assured that other men in other corporations and financial institutions, who share similar basic class interests, will do so. As Domhoff points out:

> A Property Party with two branches is one of the neatest devices ever stumbled upon by rich men determined to stay on top. It gives them a considerable flexibility, allowing them to form temporary coalitions with different elements of the underlying population as the occasion demands. It allows most of them to stay aloof from mere "partisan" political battles, only to descend on the scene from time to critical time as the high-minded civic leaders concerned with "the public interest." So one is not surprised that many wealthy businessmen play down their party affiliation, that "nonpartisan" multi-millionaires join committees to support the "best man," that Democratic and Republican money collectors can join together on numerous "bipartisan" committees for the national good, that many cor-

[1] Ferdinand Lundberg, *The Rich and the Super-Rich: A Study in the Power of Money Today,* ed. Eileen Brand (New York: Lyle Stuart, 1968), p. 41.

[2] G. William Domhoff, *Fat Cats and Democrats* (Englewood Cliffs, N.J.: Prentice-Hall, 1972).

[3] G. William Domhoff, *Who Rules America* (Englewood Cliffs, N.J.: Prentice-Hall, 1967).

porations and law firms have representatives on both sides
of the political fence, and that corporate executives give their
easily-earned monies to Republicans in one race and Democrats
in another.[4]

Domhoff's work gives sufficient documentation of this empirical claim, so that I will not attempt in this short essay to
prove the point.

None of this should be taken to suggest that the two major
parties are identical. On the contrary, there are important differences in tone and style as well as differences in which
sectors of the ruling circles generally lean towards them. The
Republican party is more attractive to the American upper
class and more likely to be forthright about its political conservatism. Its political base is primarily among the WASPs,
but it can sometimes make forays into ethnic minorities by
the right combination of racist and jingoist appeals. Its appeal
is felt most heavily, outside the ruling class, among upper-
middle-class managers, engineers, physicians and dentists,
and independent small businessmen. The Democratic party,
on the other hand, appeals to a

> . . . coalition of rich Jews, reactionary Southerners, clever cor-
> poration lawyers, and wealthy Protestant mavericks . . . [who]
> clumsily embrace each other while at the same time mollifying
> a constituency of blacks, browns, Catholics, Southerners, and
> middle-class do-gooders.[5]

These different constituencies sometimes, though by no
means always, represent a tendency on the part of one or the
other party to take the interests of its constituencies more
seriously than the other party would, within the limits of doing
nothing that would injure the primary responsibility each party
feels to the people who make America what it is: the elite of
business and finance who pay for most of the party's expenses. But even this is too strong. After all, the Democratic
party can hardly be expected to serve all of its non-ruling-
class constituencies equally, given that some of these have

[4] Domhoff, *Who Rules America*.

[5] Domhoff, *Fat Cats and Democrats*.

conflicting interests (e.g., urban blacks and rural Southern racists).

It is crucial, however, to stress the limitations on the tendency to take non-ruling-class constituencies' interests seriously. Many upper-middle-class families, who previously held illusions of power within the American system often mediated through their attachment to positions of prestige in one or the other of the two major parties, found themselves completely powerless over the Vietnam war issue when their interest (in not raising children to be killed in a war or being forced to seek refuge in Canada) was subordinated to the ruling-class interest of preserving the free world for capitalist investment. The Democratic party, despite its claim to be the vehicle for "the common man," has done an amazing job in containing movements for social change and in providing the barest minimum of social legislation necessary to prevent widespread radicalization, while doing its best to restrict any infringement on the needs of the propertied few. It is true that the Democratic party is often portrayed by its opponent as somehow favoring creeping socialism, but while this notion makes sense in a political context where Neanderthal Republicans accuse Richard Nixon of being a communist in disguise, and makes great theater, it has very little connection with any objective assessment of reality. What is true is that the Democratic party has had much better contact with the developing movements for social change, has managed to convince representatives of these movements that it is only through working in the Democratic party that their goals will be achieved, and has then come through with programs that at least addressed issues that have been on the minds of the masses. But this "addressing" of issues has almost always been stop-gap, giving far more in rhetoric than in substance.

The account given here is not meant to be a description of anyone's subjective intentions. I am not suggesting that someone once sat down, cleverly worked out a conspiracy, and then convinced all sorts of terrible people to join him in its execution. Nor am I suggesting that most politicians in the major parties perceive themselves as representatives of the American ruling class, although some certainly do. What is being suggested is that the objective consequence of a variety of institutional arrangements insures that the interests of the

American upper class, which owns and controls the productive and financial apparatus of the United States, will be served
above all else by the two major parties.[6]

Political campaigns, the previous discussion notwithstanding, are about *something*—and it does make a difference who
wins. The problem is that voters almost never get to know
what the differences are really about. For instance, there are
different sectors of the American business elite who are
closer to one party than the other and closer to one candidate
within that party than to another. While the decisions of both
parties and nearly all candidates are likely to be the same
with regard to preserving the system as a whole, they may be
quite different vis-à-vis advancing the interests of one sector
of the economy or one particular corporation as opposed to
another *within* that system. In fact, since virtually every one
who gets power in the system shares the general desire to
preserve the system and to protect the ruling class, most of
what goes under the name politics in America is really about
which section of the ruling class should be advanced through
government protection, intervention, and aid. These are not
trivial questions in a competitive economy whose main
dynamic is cutthroat competition. The answers mean the difference between survival and demise of a Lockheed or a
Boeing; hence of unemployment or employment in one area
or another for many tens of thousands of workers. Elections
do have consequences, though often not the ones that politicians talk most about when they are running for office.

[6] The existence of an American ruling class has been demonstrated
through such a variety of empirical studies in the past few years that it is
almost incredible to hear the astounded guffaws from most academics
when the term is used. Because of the important consequences that such
a position has, it is almost always impossible to use this bit of information
in any essay without transforming it into an essay about that bit of information. I refuse. If knowledge is to be cumulative and not simply repetitive,
then the burden here must be on the critic to read and to refute the
numerous studies done on this topic. To cite a few: Gabriel Kolko, *Wealth
& Power In America: An Analysis of Social Class and Income Distribution*
(New York: Praeger, 1962); Gabriel Kolko, *Roots of American Foreign
Policy: An Analysis of Power and Purpose* (Boston: Beacon Press, 1969);
Domhoff, *Who Rules America, op. cit.*; G. William Domhoff, *Higher Circles:
The Governing Class in America* (New York: Random House, 1970); Ralph
Miliband, *The State in Capitalist Society; An Analysis of the Western Sys-
tem of Power* (New York: Basic Books, 1969); Robert Fitch, *Who Rules
the Corporations?* (New York: Random House, 1973).

There is another real struggle fought out in the political arena, though again between two sections of the ruling class. It is the battle to make capitalism more rational even if that means short-term losses for the capitalist class as a whole. This phenomenon, known as corporate liberalism, results from the ability of the brightest members of the capitalist class to see that their own long-term self-interest requires changes in the short-run distribution of goods and services. While most of these corporate liberals gravitate to the Democratic party, it must be noted that there are a share of them in the Republican party as well, backing men like Javits, Case, and McCloskey. It is part of the genius of American politics that each party does seem to have its Neanderthals and its progressives and while the Neanderthals often win out, the spectacle of the battle provides better entertainment than any Roman gladiator could have done for an audience bored to tears by its sense of homogeneity everywhere it looks.

Yet, from a standpoint outside the fray, the similarities between the two parties and between sections within the parties are so apparent that the internal battles lose the weighty significance they are supposed to have for us. Now, we might expect this disenchantment in someone with a radical perspective. But what convinced me, and thousands of others like me, to take a closer look at the party system was the fact that we, *as principled liberals,* were utterly unable to find any significant difference between the parties and their factions. Our search for an explanation led inevitably to a radical analysis. Indeed the ruse of the two-party system is seen through by literally millions of Americans, most of whom never read an empirical study on the topic, and many of whom have been led by their insight either into radical political activity (the optimists) or into political quietism and apathy (the pessimists). Nor will many young people give to an electoral system that they perceive as a fraud the same energy they lavished on the antiwar movement in the 1960s.

The reason why so many people in the 1960s came to perceive the parties were fundamentally identical is that on virtually every significant political issue there seemed to be close accord between the two parties. The Great Consensus politics engineered by Lyndon Johnson may have had a short ideological reign, but the substance of consensus politics sustained itself through the 1960s strongly enough so that even by the 1970 congressional election there were very few seats at stake where any really substantive political issue was being debated. But how is this possible? Certainly the underlying nature of the Property party does not explain this adequately. After all, the different branches of the party are real, and if the party is to function well, its Democratic branch must appear to represent the interests of labor, even if it does not do so with too much vigor or aggressiveness. Why didn't the Democratic party have to maintain more clearly its ideological distinctions, and launch more apparent forays in the interests of working people? The answer to this question may help us to see more clearly what the causal factors will be that will determine the future of the two-party system.

In brief, the answer is this: Republicans and Democrats are allowed to appear alike, without basically undermining the smooth functioning of the Property party, when people have the lowest degree of class consciousness and hence when the particular interests of the ruling class as a whole can be sold as the general interests of all society. It is the waning of the class struggle in America that makes all sorts of open collaboration possible not only between "the party of labor" and "the party of big business," but even between the leader of labor and the bosses themselves. The period in history in which this occurred, roughly the postwar period, was one in which it suddenly appeared as if all the contradictions had been solved, history had come to an end, and the great American dream had finally been realized for most white Americans. The good life was at hand, prosperity and suburbia for all. If this means loneliness in the crowd, it also meant an end to ideology and a beginning of the great celebration of the American present. Management and labor could work together in a framework of essential harmony to solve some of the remaining problems. What remained to be solved could be handled with a little bit of social engineering, a little bit of guts, and an awful lot of plain old-fashioned patience.

It was all made possible by the emergence of the United States after World War II as the world's leading imperialist power. The United States was the only major industrial country to emerge from the war with its productive capacities unscathed and its military might increased by the war. The other competition for capitalist world domination (from Japan, Germany, France, and Britain) had been devastated; and

Russia, although potent in its rhetorical significance as justifying the cold war policies, took a decade before it could recover from its 20 million war dead and its tremendous economic losses. As the world's most powerful economic power, the United States could and did write the terms of trade with all the other countries of the world. Its currency became the universal equivalent in place of gold. As the economic empires of Britain and France began to topple, U.S. industries, often assisted directly by foreign-aid programs, moved in to take over.[7]

In concrete terms, U.S. imperialism meant a number of crucial things for the American economy. First, it meant that the United States could impose a pattern of development on the Third World countries that suited the needs of American business. What this often meant was that a Third World country was forced to maintain a one- or two-crop economy dominated by foreign investors. Industrialization was often either prevented or channeled into fields that would not be competitive with major U.S. interests in that area. For the imperialized country, of course, this meant permanent imposed underdevelopment.[8] Second, U. S. imperialism meant that the United States could exploit the raw materials of a particular country without fairly compensating the inhabitants of the country. Copper from Chile and offshore oil from Vietnam made attractive booty for the large corporations who could make large profits from selling the world's common inheritance for private gain. Third, the United States could invest in enterprises around the world and set its own terms in countries that were starved for enough capital to get back onto their feet economically. While much focus has been given in recent years to the effects of U. S. imperialism in the Third World, it must also be stressed that U. S. capital played an important role in rebuilding the capitalist markets in Europe, and that U. S. investors made large sums of money by having these markets for investment open to them that previously would have been dominated by European capital.[9]

[7] A more detailed account of this development can be found in David Horowitz's *The Free World Colossus* (New York: Hill & Wang, 1963).

[8] See Paul Mattick, *Marx and Keynes: The Limits of the Mixed Economy* (Boston: Porter Sargent, 1969).

[9] See Harry Magdoff, *Age of Imperialism: The Economics of U.S. Foreign Policy* (New York: Monthly Review Press, 1969).

What all this meant for the American economy cannot be overestimated. The Great Depression was not ended, as liberals like to suppose, by the New Deal. On the contrary, as an economic measure, the New Deal really failed to meet the problem. It was preparation for war, including lend-lease, that moved the economy out of the stalemate of the 1930s. It was the cold war and U. S. imperialism, which the cold war was designed to serve, that kept the United States from falling back into it. Dean Acheson made this point clearly in his testimony before the special Congressional Committee on Postwar Economic Policy and Planning, when he warned that the only way to avoid another depression would be to ensure that we have adequate foreign markets:

> You don't have a problem of production. The United States has unlimited creative energy. The important thing is markets. . . . We could argue for quite a while that under a different system in this country you could use the entire production of the country in the United States . . . you find you must look to other markets and those markets are broad. . . . If I am wrong about that, then all the argument falls by the wayside, but my contention is that we cannot have full employment and prosperity in the United States without the foreign markets.[10]

U. S. petroleum earnings on investments in Latin America, between 1956 and 1968, after local taxes, were 20.5 percent.

> In 1961 the foreign subsidiaries of the Aluminum Corporation of America generated 65% of its net income, 80% of Yale & Towne's net earnings, 78% of Colgate Palmolive's profits, 35% of Corn Products' Sales, and 48% of Pfizer's total volume. Forty-four of the one hundred top US industrial corporations in the same year were no less dependent on their overseas branches for sales and profits.[11]

It is sometimes argued that because foreign investment is less than 10 percent of domestic capital investment and because total exports are less than 5 percent of the gross national product, it cannot be the case that they are crucial in the American economy. GNP, first of all, is an expanded

[10] U.S., Congress, House, Hearings Before the Special Subcommittee on Postwar Economic Policy and Planning, 78th Cong., 2d sess., 1944.

[11] Kolko, Roots of American Foreign Policy, op. cit., pp. 76–77.

figure that includes governmental expenditures; activities of banks, real estate firms, and stock brokers; and trade. As Harry Magdoff points out, if we exclude these and just focus on "the business of farms, factories and mines, . . . foreign business amounts to quite a noteworthy volume relative to the internal market."[12] Profit from the Third World plays a crucial role in the life of domestic nonfinancial corporations, in 1964 accounting for about 22 percent of all their profits. And this is on the increase.

> For example, in manufacturing industries during the past ten years, domestic sales increased by 50% while foreign sales by US owned factories increased over 110%. Thus, as far as the commodity-producing industries are concerned, foreign markets have become a major sphere of economic interest and have proven to be increasingly important to US businesses as an offset to the stagnating tendencies of the inner market.[13]

What's more, though the superprofits made in the Third World do not always represent the major portion of profits for a given corporation, these profits are often essential in raising the general profit level of a corporation to a point where the firm is making enough to stay solvent or return something to the investors. Generally, a firm must reach a certain level of productive activity before it can make a profit. Costs of depreciation of machinery, use of plants, costs of administration remain constant at a given level of capacity—so the firm must sell enough goods to meet the overhead or it will lose money. What Third World investments and markets often do is to provide the margin through which the firm can start to go beyond the break-even point and make much profit.

What does all this have to do with class struggle in the United States? In the period during which the United States gained ascendency in worldwide imperialism, it was able to "soak out" of the peoples of the world tremendous wealth, most of which was brought back to the United States to fill the coffers of the super-rich, but some of which "trickled down" to the working class to meet the demands for a higher standard of material comfort. More precisely, with superprofits available to the rich, it was possible to raise the pay of work-

[12] Magdoff, *op. cit.,* p. 178.

[13] *Ibid.,* pp. 183–184.

ers without cutting into their own wealth. So an apparent
coincidence of interests occurred between large sections of
the working class and the rulers. (I say large sections,
because even when imperialism was in its heyday, it still did
not rectify the inequalities within the working class, the discrimination against minority groups, and the oppression of
women, but rather sustained all of these. In fact, many minority groups were living in conditions identical to those that
white workers faced in the depths of the depression.) In this
period, the class struggle that Marx had predicted would be a
permanent feature of the internal life of capitalist nations was
transferred to the international sphere. It became more accurate to speak of a class struggle between the advanced industrial imperialist societies, on the one hand, and the under-
developed colonialized societies, on the other. Even within the
colonial societies the same development was paralleled, the
peasantry and proletariat often merged with elements of the
bourgeoisie to participate in national liberation struggles based
on a coalition of classes.

So the condition for the emergence of the great consensus
in America was the unchallenged hegemony of the American
economic machine throughout the world. As long as the system delivered a high level of material comfort, at least for an
important section of the working class, the edge could be
taken off the class struggle. Workers did not feel that they
had all they ever would need, but it seemed as though America
could solve the basic problems of the economy so that most
of what one needed could be gotten through the system if
one worked hard, got liberals elected to office, and moderately
reformed those aspects of the system one did not like. The
apparent success of the system made it seem ridiculous, if
not positively suspect, to push hard for class demands and to
ask basic questions.

It was in this context that liberal and conservative labels
seemed to lose all their meaning. The liberals had emerged
from the depression with an economic program that was the
same program that Hitler had used in Germany, that is, to
build up the military and expand outward. The conservatives
naturally acquiesced in this, so the only argument was over
who was doing a better job. Politics was concerned with
which tactics could best preserve and expand America's
economic empire, which seemed to be benefiting all (though,

to be sure—but wasn't that just fair in a free society—some more than others). So President Kennedy rode to fame over an alleged missile-gap he made up in order to scare people into thinking that only by spending more on defense could we possibly catch up with the (mythical) advances of the Russians. Even Eugene McCarthy argued against the war in Vietnam on the grounds that it misspent resources that could better be used to defend U. S. strength in Europe and Latin America.

Once we understand the crucial role that American economic imperialism played in defining the nature of American politics in the postwar period, we can see why the Vietnam war was a turning point and why the period ahead is likely to be decisively different. The Vietnam war is being fought to defend American imperialism around the globe. Those who defended the war and planned it made it very clear that what was at stake was not just Vietnam itself, whose economic importance might be negligible, but the security of the entire American empire. If a small and weak people like the Vietnamese could take control of their own economic life, then that message would spread to Latin America and Africa as well, and the dominoes would begin to fall. Only some stupid politicians vulgarized this theory into a vision of Red Chinese troops marching into Canada or Venezuela. But as originally enunciated by the sophisticated McNamara-Rusk-Bundy crew, it was a theory that was correct in the essentials. What is important for us to understand, after the war has dragged on for over ten years, is that the war has not been won by the United States, and that the prediction of danger turned out to be *self-fulfilling.*

The Vietnam war helped to stir up forces that were already brewing in America. Even when U. S. imperialism was working well, there were several groups that were not really satisfied with what America had to offer. First, there were blacks, Chicanos, and American Indians, who had never "bought into" the American dream and who had never been allowed to lead the kind of close-to-affluent lives held out to white workers. Racism may well have been instituted and sustained for economic reasons, but it had taken on a life of its own in the ideological sphere which made it very difficult for blacks even to fantasize some kind of "normal" life in America. In response to that racism, the blacks had already launched a movement

for civil rights. But it was only with the advent of severe
escalation of the war in Vietnam and consequent downgrading
of domestic spending that it became apparent to most blacks
that the high-sounding rhetoric of racial justice was not to be
matched with any real action. The Vietnam war thus aggra-
vated a preexisting problem.

Second, there were large numbers of young people who had
passed through affluence and found it wanting. These were
the sons and daughters of the people who had struggled out
of the depression piggyback on the peoples of the world, and
found that the world created for them by their parents was
basically alienating and unfulfilling. "I can't get no satisfaction,
and I try, and I try" went the words of an extremely popular
song of the 1960s. That theme reverberated throughout an
entire generation of young people who were fed up with
"plastic" America. This feeling did not begin with the war.
The large student demonstrations began before the Vietnam
war had made much of an impression on their consciousness,
and while the sharp escalation of the war and the draft calls
undoubtedly helped intensify this feeling, it is nonetheless
surprising how many of the people who developed the counter-
culture of the late 1960s were not activists or people primarily
concerned with the war.

Third, there was the reawakening of the women's movement
against sexist institutions and male chauvinist practices. The
movement had gained impetus from the realization by women
in the antiwar movement that for even the most advanced and
politically conscious men, chauvinism was integral to their
being and would not be eliminated until women organized
separately around their own needs.

The war created none of these forces: they are endemic in
the capitalist structure of American society. But the war
helped give them momentum to a point where they became
serious movements on their own, unlikely to disappear or
move back to the relatively low level of visibility that they
had before the escalation of the war. The Vietnam war had a
catalytic effect in developing the consciousness of opposi-
tional elements in the United States, but its most important
effect was to weaken the hold of American imperialism around
the world—not ironically, by precipitating a series of other
colonial rebellions, but by draining U. S. gold reserves and
causing runaway inflation. While the attention of the country

was turned entirely to Southeast Asia, the reemergence of Germany and Japan as serious economic competitors was completely ignored. Perhaps the American capitalists so completely assumed their own racial superiority that they refused to believe that Japan could ever rival the United States in technological expertise; perhaps the capitalists, fooled by their own rhetoric, actually began to believe that the communist menace was everywhere and accounted for everything. Certainly some "enlightened" capitalists saw the "danger" coming and tried to warn people (notably, for example, Senator Mansfield). But by and large, the idea that the United States could ever be seriously challenged in the economic realm never really occurred to public consciousness until it was a fact. By 1971 the United States was no longer running the world with unchallenged economic hegemony.

I am *not* suggesting that suddenly, overnight, the United States is no longer number one. It is, and may well remain that for many years to come. But what is over, decisively and for the foreseeable future, is the ability of the United States to dictate its own terms around the world by facing no real competition for markets. Even within the United States itself, trade barriers may have to be resorted to in order to stop Japanese and German goods from underselling American manufacturers. We have returned to the pre-World-War-II period in which the competition among advanced capitalist societies played a crucial role in the internal development of these societies.

The consequences of this transition will be felt increasingly strongly within the United States. If the ability to profit from the rest of the world is to be limited in the period ahead, then someone is going to have to lose out. And presumably it will not be the American ruling class, who will attempt to pass any new hardships on to the working class. When faced with limits on its maneuverability, the ruling class will generally opt for tightening the belts of workers. The current wage/price-freeze policy is a good example. The runaway inflation is caused by the war and by unbounded profiteering of capitalists. Yet, when controls are instituted, they apply only to income that is earned, but not at all to unearned income from stocks, bonds, and dividends. Controls on wages are closely supervised; prices, however, face relatively easy sailing, particularly when a manufacturer can introduce new products.

Lest anyone think that higher wages caused the inflation, consider that in the period 1965–1969 wages rose 14.4 percent, while prices rose 15.5 percent, and profits rose 30.2 percent. As things get tighter, due to the change in America's position, on the international scene, it will increasingly be the workers who are forced to pay.

Needless to say, I am not suggesting that American imperialism is washed up or that the empire is on the verge of collapse. I am attempting to develop a conceptual model that can illuminate our experience and indicate the direction in which things may likely move. We are trying to describe dynamic realities. At any moment one feature of that reality is likely to be more dominant than another, but this is not to imply that the reality only has that one feature. It is my contention that in the period of the next twelve years the conflict between the advanced capitalist societies will play a much larger role than it has played in the past twenty years, that America's economic hegemony will be severely limited, and that the resultant economic squeeze will radicalize a working class that has been relatively dormant in the post-World-War-II period.

II

Assuming that my scenario for the period ahead is right in most of its particulars, it is inevitable that the radicalized segments of the working class will seek political expression. And that is likely to have an important impact on the party system. Probably the most immediate effect will be the reintroduction of ideological rhetoric by the spokesmen of the parties. For instance, we will hear more from the Democrats about the common man and more appeals from the Republicans to abandon sectional interests and to return to the bipartisan politics without which the national interest cannot be served (of course, this latter phrase will be part of the ideological baggage of the Democrats if *they* should win control of the administration in 1972). The return to a partisan approach to political issues, dominated by ideological categories, need not, however, bespeak any transformation in the real interests or actions of the parties. Harry Truman, one of the engineers of the cold war, was popular as a fighter against the big guys, including the big corporations. Many of the New Deal Democrats, including LBJ himself, voiced a seemingly radical line on corporations in the 1930s—it made for good home consumption among a population fed up with a capitalist society but not exactly knowing how to move. Indeed, America has a rich history of populism; that history can always be called upon and to some extent revived by the Democratic party when it suits the times.

Nor is it likely to stop there. There will certainly be some attempt by liberal elements of the Democratic party to develop a program that can speak to the developing crisis in American society. Such a program, kept in the wings until the mainstream elements in the party are convinced that it is absolutely essential to run with it, will undoubtedly be the focus of much agitation among youth by the Democratic party loyalists: "Here, work for this and the whole society can be reformed from within."

But it is not at all obvious what such a program could include. After all, it was the liberals in the Democratic party who called for wage-price controls in 1971 and who were astounded when President Nixon used them. True, the liberals can now call for a fairer system of controls, with profit and dividend controls, but that is not for long going to be perceived as a real alternative, even by the liberals who will be trying to head off any grass-roots labor rebellion. Equally important, virtually any solution likely to emerge from either party at this time or in the near future will be one that, insofar as it attempts to cater to the needs of working people, will pit those needs against the needs of the least powerful sections of the working class, including the nonunionized, minority groups, and the poor. This conflict will be fought primarily in the area of the budget: necessary services, talked about but never delivered, will be postponed once again. The working class will be told that it is being taken advantage of by people looking for a handout and that it must choose between social legislation, which would entail a heavier tax burden, and no social legislation.

The tactic of pitting working people against poor and deprived peoples is a constant theme in American politics, even when imperialism is doing relatively well. The emergence of a Conservative party in New York points to one possible direction that a new coalition of forces could go. The most reactionary elements in the Republican party, often composed of well-to-do upper-middle-class businessmen and some professionals who for a variety of reasons feel extremely insecure and marginal in the economy, put forward an explicitly racist alliance that plays on the fears of working-class people by showing them that every gain made by the poor will be at the expense of working people. And the Conservatives are right; because as things are now set up, every advance of the poor or black people will be at the expense of working people. The ruling class certainly is not going to be willing to bear the burden itself when it can shift that burden to the workers instead. Nevertheless, this new coalition, which is likely to be increasingly popular, may very quickly be co-opted by opportunist elements in both major parties, undermining the ability of a third-party force to do much with it. In part, this is a building block of Nixon's Southern strategy. It is a strategy unlikely to tear the major parties apart, precisely because many elements in both parties can and will play to it. And it will be given an added dimension as economic nationalism becomes more important as a device for dealing with foreign competition. But it will not split the parties or cause major realignment precisely because both parties can compete over who is doing a better job of keeping law and order, whose program really is more sensitive to the desire of working people not to be burdened by the poor, and who is most concerned with protecting American workers and American business from the threat from abroad.

Such an alliance will put liberals in the Democratic party in bad shape—since they have traditionally championed the black, the poor, etc., within the context of respectable dissent. Increasingly, they will be pushed by their constituencies to find some other vehicle for political action. Genuine ideological liberals will find it increasingly easy to join hands, as they are beginning to do now, with a section of the ruling class that has heavy investments in the cities and believes that more spending around the cities is the only way to save their investments. These corporate fat cats are increasingly interested in programs for ecology, housing (Ford Motor Company, for instance, has a plan to make a fortune through factory-produced housing units), and general distribution of funds to the ghettos. Under a liberal banner, the idea runs, we could construct a coalition of young people, who are antiwar and who would support domestic spending of the current military budget, of poor and black people, and an important section of the corporate elite. Such a coalition might even be vaguely populist, using anti-business rhetoric to support its ecological programs. The vanguard of such an alliance might be John Gardner's Common Cause or the forces that are gathering around Ralph Nader.

Unfortunately for the liberals, this kind of a coalition does not speak to the major problem of the 1970s, the decline in United States worldwide economic hegemony. Insofar as it hangs together, the coalition depends on a strategy that counterposes the interests of workers to those of the poor and simply sides with the poor, the blacks, the young, etc. But insofar as it seeks alliances with an increasingly militant section of the working class, it would be forced to focus on the questions of who runs the economy and who benefits. Once it does that, it will drive away its source of financial support and legitimacy; that is, the corporate liberals who do not really want to call into question their whole system. So the liberal coalition has no real viability for the 1970s.[14]

Nevertheless, it will undoubtedly be tried. And it is likely to be an important focus of energy and attention in the 1970s. Its key question, internally, will be whether to split from the Democratic party, and that question will not be argued simply on left-right kinds of considerations. In fact, some of the more militant sections of the coalition will want to remain inside the Democratic party because they will feel that being there will give them a legitimacy and cover from being called communists. And some of the more conservative elements of the coalition may want to break with the party, in part because they believe that the threat of such a break, if seen as real, may give them more bargaining power with their colleagues, even if they are forced to come back.

What is crucial, it seems to me, is not whether or not there will be a liberal force that emerges in the 1970s, but that such a coalition, contained or not within the Democratic party, will have no viability. Its most likely consequence will be to drive some elements of labor even further into the hands of the right wing. The increasingly radicalized sectors of the working class will not be able to relate to it until it comes up with a

---

[14] It may be an important step in the development of forces that will join the socialist party whose existence I discuss below.

real alternative to the economic philosophy of the Property party. And that is precisely what a liberal party can never do.

III

The change in America's imperial fortunes, then, is likely to change the character (though not necessarily the names) of America's political geography. I leave till last the most speculative part of my account. It seems reasonable to believe that the economic crisis ahead is likely to produce, within the next twelve years, a reemergence of a serious socialist party with an explicitly pro-working-class and anti-capitalist perspective. Such a socialist party would offer a program that spoke to the economic crisis by posing a new economic system capable of providing for people's material needs and needs for non-alienating labor, a program that spoke to the interests of blacks, of minority groups, of ecologists, of antiwar forces, and of the young. It would initially attract the most militant sections of the working class, but it would almost certainly sink deeper roots in every sector of the working class as the policies of the major Property party spoke less and less to people's real needs. I do not predict that the party that will emerge between now and 1984 would in fact lead us to socialism—only that it would offer that as a real possibility.[15]

The precondition for the emergence of such an explicitly socialist party would be the development of a left that synthesized the best elements of Old and New Left and rejected the worst aspects of both. While I cannot possibly discuss this question in detail, there are certain points that stand out. The great advantage of the Old Left was its ability to speak to the interests of large numbers of Americans and relate to their problems. The great disadvantage of the Old Left was that in its major organizational form, the Communist party, it was not an American left, but rather an agent of the Soviet Union. This fact, oft-repeated by red-baiters, but true nevertheless, meant that in a very real sense the Communist party betrayed the American working class (which in part explains the hostility

---

[15] This is not to suggest that socialism in America could be built that quickly, but that a party capable of eventually leading us to socialism could be built in the next twelve years. This would be a tremendous advance over the lack of organization that has characterized the left.

so many workers came to feel toward it). The best known instance of this was the constant change in line on foreign policy, particularly vis-à-vis the Nazis, which made it impossible to believe in the intellectual honesty of the left. But equally profound from the standpoint of the American working class was the policy of class collaboration that the Communist party pursued throughout the period of its strength. The Communist party, having as its primary interest the defense of Russia, followed a strategy of building a united front against fascism. What this meant for the American party was that it sought some kind of harmony with the liberal, pro-civil-liberties and pro-human-freedoms section of the American ruling class. Now, they reasoned, you cannot have an alliance with people if you are simultaneously stirring up their workers to rebel and take the factories away. The capitalists simply won't stand for that. So, you have to soft-pedal the class struggle and fight for liberal issues that you have a common basis of fighting for with the liberals. The extent to which the Communist party went to follow this strategy was incredible: from voting no-strike pledges during the war to finally dissolving the party itself to show they were no longer a threat. Politically, this meant that the Communist party became a staunch supporter öf Roosevelt and the backbone of the Democratic party, providing it with some of its best precinct workers. Needless to say, a party that so completely abandoned the proletariat was abandoned in turn by it. The socialist party that will emerge in the next twelve years must be a party that is rooted in the traditions of America, and the agent of the American proletariat.

The great strength of the New Left was its honesty, openness, and willingness to struggle and take great risks for what it knew to be right. Its mistakes included:

1. *Misuse and overglorification of the Third World.* The New Left was correct to reject the kind of national chauvinism that led many to support U.S. foreign policy even when they could plainly see that it was wrong. The understandable reaction was to reject all of the chauvinist nonsense and to begin to show people that the United States was doing wrong in Vietnam and in many other places around the world, that it was acting just as every other imperialist power had acted in the past, and that in fact it was being beaten on the battlefield by the Vietcong. The movement also stressed, correctly, the

humanity and beauty of the Vietnamese people. But sometimes these tendencies have gone overboard and portrayed
Third World revolutions as the embodiments of all virtue
and wisdom.

Instead of learning what was relevant, while carefully recognizing the differences between a revolution in a peasant
society and a revolution in an advanced industrial society,
many sections of the movement have attempted to mechani-
cally transplant the messages of the Third World to this
country. Hence the development of quasi-Maoist sects, who
tried to fit the American experience into a Chinese mold, and
the more general glorification of the Vietnamese and Cubans.
Such an approach left people totally confused when Mao's
China suddenly made coexistence overtures to the United
States or when it supported a dictatorship in Pakistan which
is engaged in genocide against a popular rebellion, just as it
left them confused when Cuba was forced in order to survive
(under conditions that could not foster genuine socialism) to
make accommodations with the Soviet Union that limited
internal democracy and self-determination.

The strategy for building socialism in a country with an
educated working class and a fully developed technological
and industrial base will be quite different from what is appropriate for Cuba, China, or Vietnam. The new socialist party
must make this point clear.

2. *Anti-intellectualism.* Partly in an effort to appear to be
genuinely American, and partly as a real reflection of the anti-
intellectualism of American life, many sections of the movement tended to glorify spontaneity and feeling at the expense
of, rather than alongside of, intellectual life. Feeling has often
replaced thinking; few people really come to understand that
those feelings themselves are products of an intricate process
of education and socialization—not something pure and "natural" that has been polluted by thought and reflection. Instead
of making a careful study of America, the movement has been
quick to adopt slogans and fads that are not only implausible,
but often mutually self-contradictory. Inconsistency itself
became a glorified principle, mistakenly confused with "dialec-
tical thinking."

The most destructive fad adopted in recent years has been
that of the street-fighting urban guerrilla. Some sections of
the movement have established a criterion of seriousness that

revolved around how many crazy risks one is willing to take and how much one is in the street fighting. But the real areas where militancy is needed—the struggles for power in each community and each institution—were often seen as somehow reformist. The notion was that anything short of the final revolutionary battle is impure, so count us out until the golden moment arrives. If there is to be an advance beyond the 1960s, this silly romanticism and pretending that we are all really Third World guerrillas must be squarely rejected.

3. *Inwardness.* The impetus toward self-transformation that developed in the movement in the past few years was rooted in a justifiable reaction to some of the worst aspects of previous movement practice. The movement was almost as alienating as the rest of society in many respects. Competition for approval and power often seemed to be the dominant mode; meetings often turned into furious ego-battles between aggressive males. Women were often relegated to the same kind of menial work they were assigned in the rest of the society, and made to feel that their insights and understanding were too inferior to be worth mouthing to the "heavies." In a similar way, nonaggressive men were shoved aside if they had not mastered the same verbal skills that gave the "superstars" their visibility and power.

Everyone felt stifled and used, and as a result, the movement had an even larger turnover in membership than its essentially transient student population would have dictated. In this context, basic rethinking of the way people related to each other was absolutely essential. But some sections of the movement were so concerned with the task of transforming the consciousness of their own members that they began to ignore the plight of the rest of the population. Fantasies began to emerge that everyone could reject his whole conditioning immediately upon realizing the problem and beginning to struggle against it. The notion somehow developed that movement activists not only could, but must, transform themselves into socialist human beings before the revolution. This utopian ideal actually created the reverse of what it sought. In the name of making relationships in the movement more humane and less based on authority figures and male chauvinism, some sections of the movement have focused on fighting itself and become more inhumane and less sensitive. A socialist movement of the period ahead would have to be a movement whose primary aim was in reaching a majority of Americans with the ideas of socialism and how to achieve it.

4. *Anti-Leadership.* Part of the reason for this in the New Left was the unresponsiveness of the leadership that emerged in the 1960s to many of the real interests of people who came into the New Left. Another part, however, was the unjustified feeling that since the goal was for everyone to control his or her own life, the goal should be realizable immediately: hence everyone should be a leader. A socialist movement in America must have leadership that is public, democratically elected, and replaceable easily when people are dissatisfied with it. Stalinism must be completely rejected. But so too must the anarchistic approach to leadership that so often leads to elitism and dishonesty—because leadership does get provided, but then it has to deny that it is leadership and begin to lead by dishonest methods.

What encourages me to believe that a left force could actually develop? Two things. First it is possible to learn from the past. Young people are coming to realize the mistakes of the past and are attempting to correct them. Second, we are entering a period in which many working people are being driven to the left by virtue of the circumstances of American capitalism. Many of the mistakes of the New Left were strongly related to the fact that the movement of the 1960s was largely based on middle-class students. Those mistakes are less likely to be made by a working class more in touch with the day-to-day realities that emerge in the struggle for survival.

The emergence, between now and 1984, of a real socialist party, seriously contending for power around its programs, would have a very profound effect on the political landscape. For the first few years of its existence, it would be ignored by the media—except when it was given credit for disruptions of internal American stability (undoubtedly, prison revolts, militant demonstrations, bombings, and so forth, would all be attributed to it and we would be reminded frequently of how calm America would be if only there were no socialist party). But after a while the seriousness of such a party would force a more political response, and it is not unlikely that the response would be a serious realignment of the two major parties along ideological lines in such a way that the Democratic party would begin to sound as if it were really interested in everything the socialist party wanted, except that it would not want to move too quickly in the direction of ending capitalism. That is, a real socialist party would inevitably push the focus of political debate in this country far to the left, at least to the point where political discussion began to resemble that of European countries in which social-democratic parties have existed for a long time. Inevitably, the socialist party would have a left wing and a right wing, with the latter insisting that if only the party tempered what it said a little bit it could win elections, the former stressing the need to prepare for other forms of political activity besides just the electoral form, for example, general strikes, militant demonstrations, and possibly even insurrection. Exactly which side would win out would inevitably be determined by a variety of factors that cannot be predicted here, ranging from economic circumstances to the quality of leadership on each side of the dispute.

Any philosopher must feel particularly uneasy about writing an account of what will happen in the future. Even determinists believe that the future can be foretold only in principle, saving for God the actual ability to know in advance all the causal factors that will yield a particular future occurrence. For someone like myself, who is not a determinist, the ability to write this essay is even more problematic. The most important element determining the future, it seems to me, will be human choices. There is no way to say for sure what choices human beings will make, because human beings, unlike plants, have the ability to transcend their previous conditioning and make choices on the basis of their understanding of what ought to be the case.

Still, as Marx taught us, human beings make their own history but in circumstances which are not of their own choosing. And it is certainly the case that once a certain set of decisions are made, there are certain regularities in behavior of large enough magnitude so that we can safely predict some kinds of societal developments. What I have been attempting in this essay is to describe the context in which people will be making the decisions about how to act politically.

But it is precisely because human beings are free that it does make sense to engage in the present enterprise. Because the prediction of where things may be going or could be going itself becomes a factor in determining the future. There is no better example of this than in the history of Marx's own work. The fact that Marx made clear to the bourgeoisie what the key weaknesses of their system were made it possible for some of them to take important steps temporarily to alleviate some of the worst aspects of capitalist oppression and hence to give a new lease on life to the capitalist order. Conversely, it is by seeing that there are real possibilities for a different social order that people are inspired to take risks in order to achieve it. It is in this latter spirit that I offer my prognosis of the years ahead: in the understanding that the political parties that have for so long dominated American political life need not dominate the political life of the next twelve years. The Property party can be faced by a genuine People's party that is for socialism. Whether this will happen or not largely depends on the choices that we make.

IRA KATZNELSON

is Assistant Professor of Political Science at Columbia University and Research Associate at the Center for Policy Research. He is the editor of *Politics and Society,* a journal founded in 1970 as an alternative to the prevailing paucity of critical analysis and depoliticization of the study of politics. His book *Black Men, White Cities* will be published by Oxford University Press in late 1972.

---

urban
counterrevolution

"Time has run out," John Lindsay has written. "Our cities will either be saved—now—or they will not be saved at all."[1] But saved for whom? It is fashionable to inquire whether our cities will survive the "urban crisis." The language of crisis, however, has a pseudo-neutral vocabulary, usually spoken by technocrats who neglect to ask, "Whose crisis?"[2] By contrast, revolutionary rhetoric, in spite of its hyperbole, is fundamental and precise: "Whose revolution?" is the core of its message. Crises are managed; revolutions won or repressed. And in present-day America, those who manage seek to repress.

From the perspective of political and economic elites, there is an urban crisis, not because the air is foul, the transit network hopelessly inadequate, or the prisons places of custodial

[1] John V. Lindsay, *The City* (New York: New American Library, 1970), p. 218.
[2] This is not to deny that serious challenges of "crisis" proportions face urban America. But it is to say that the terms used to describe that challenge have implications for the analysis of the causes and for the political stance that one adopts.

brutality; rather, the crisis is one of legitimacy, stability, and social control. The expressive ghetto rebellions of the 1960s indicated an unexpected depth of estrangement. The situation at the end of the decade could not yet be characterized as revolutionary (the protests were too inchoate and lacking in leadership and organization to be that). Yet, if acute multiple dislocations, systemic contradictions, and a rapid development of collective political consciousness are the symptoms and causes of *pre*revolutionary situations, at the end of the 1960s urban America entered a prerevolutionary period of uncertain duration and resolution.

Prerevolutionary situations are also pre*counter*revolutionary situations. Arno J. Mayer notes:

> Obviously, revolution and counterrevolution are two inseparable sides of one and the same refractory historical constellation. But more often than not, incumbent elites and institutions successfully control or crush convulsive disruptions. . . . In any case, crisis situations have a double-edged nature and impulse. Excessive preoccupation with their revolutionary aspects has contributed to the relative neglect of their equally essential and dialectically linked counterrevolutionary facets.[3]

It is the contention of this essay that the prerevolutionary rebellions of the 1960s have occasioned an anticipatory counterrevolution[4] that seeks to defuse urban conflict, restore trust in the political system, and conserve the essentials of the status quo. The urban counterrevolution is well underway, if ill-understood. It has an ideology and a program. And if it succeeds, it will impose on our cities a soft version of 1984, in the beneficent guise of liberal, participatory reform.

I

The ghetto rebellions were profoundly political. Their targets —white-owned property and the police—were visible symbols of public authority and political and economic legitimacy. The disorders have been realistically compared to "native" upris-

---

[3] Arno J. Mayer, *Dynamics of Counterrevolution in Europe, 1870–1956: An Analytic Framework* (New York: Harper & Row, 1971), pp. 46–47.

[4] The term is used slightly differently by Mayer, *Ibid.,* p. 104 ff. Here I refer to elite attempts to forestall the development of a prerevolutionary situation into a revolutionary one. Their counterrevolutionary actions anticipate this development.

ings against oppressive, colonial-like relationships.[5] If the key contemporary components of the internal colonial dynamic in the United States are racism ("a principle of social domination by which a group seen as inferior or different in terms of alleged biological characteristics is exploited, controlled, and oppressed socially and psychically by a superordinate group"), cultural deracination, and administration by representatives of the dominant power,[6] the rebellions (seen as powerful pleas for domestic decolonization) revealed an anticolonial, and potentially anticapitalist, revolutionary potential. And, by implication, they indicated the extent to which the breakdown of urban political machines threatened elite interests.

The political machine was an ideal instrument of elite protection. From an elite vantage point, the entry of new groups into politics is unsettling. The manner in which the newcomers are linked to the political system affects the continuity and stability of existing arrangements. Thus Samuel P. Huntington asserts in his handbook for "creating order in changing societies" that where "groups gain entry into politics without becoming identified with the established political organizations or acquiescing in the established political procedures," the system's structured patterns of dominance cannot "stand up against the impact of a new social force." The essential issue is the extent to which the "system is protected by mechanisms that restrict and moderate the impact of new groups," either by slowing down their entry into politics or by impelling changes in the attitudes and behavior of the group's most politically active members.[7]

The machine performed these elite supportive insulating functions. It flourished in the United States in the late nineteenth and early twentieth centuries in a period of convulsive social change, urban growth, and massive migration of European peasants, who "required the most extensive acculturation simply to come to terms with urban industrial existence as such, much less to enter the party system as relatively

---

[5] See Robert Blauner, "Whitewash over Watts," *Transaction* 3 (March/April 1966), 3–9, and Robert Allen, *Black Awakening in White Capitalist America* (Garden City, N.Y.: Doubleday, 1970), pp. 4–88.

[6] Robert Blauner, "Internal Colonialism and Ghetto Revolt," *Social Problems,* 16 (Spring 1969), pp. 393 ff.

[7] Samuel P. Huntington, *Political Order In Changing Societies* (New Haven, Conn.: Yale University Press, 1968), pp. 88–89.

independent actors."[8] It is often noted that the machine form served the immigrants well. Less often remarked on is the machine's conservative nature. Machine politicians acted as buffers between their clientele and dominant elites. "Frequently, a three-cornered relationship developed in which the machine politician could be viewed as a broker who, in return for financial assistance from wealthy elites, promoted their policy interests while in office, while passing along a portion of the gain to a particularistic electorate from whom he 'rented' his authority."[9] By its lack of a class orientation, its emphasis on short-run gains at the expense of fundamental transformations, and its reinforcement of the legitimacy of existing arrangements by wedding the immigrant to the political system by providing concrete rewards, the machine represented an alternative to violence in a social setting where the potential for violence was high.

The mass migration of blacks to the North in this century has taken place in two stages, divided by the depression years: 1900–1930, when approximately 1.5 million blacks left the South; and 1940 to the present, when 4 million more came to the cities. The black migrants were incorporated into the polity in the earlier period by the cities' machines, albeit on terms that differed considerably from those the European immigrants fashioned. In New York City, for example, Tammany Hall established a black auxiliary, the United Colored Democracy, as the city-wide Democratic party organization for blacks. Unlike the other, largely ethnically homogeneous Tammany clubs, the UCD lacked a territorial base; its leaders were selected by the party's white leadership, not by the black community. As a result of this arrangement, black powerlessness was the norm for the generation that settled Harlem. As late as 1935, when Harlem's population was over 95 percent black, the area had white Democratic district leaders who presided over virtually segregated political clubs.[10]

[8] Walter Dean Burnham, "Party Systems and the Political Process," in William Nisbet Chambers and Walter Dean Burnham (eds.), *The American Party Systems: Stages of Political Development* (New York: Oxford University Press, 1967), p. 286.

[9] James C. Scott, "Corruption, Machine Politics, and Political Change," *American Political Science Review*, 63 (December 1969), pp. 1154 ff.

[10] For an extended discussion, see Ira Katznelson, *Black Men, White Cities* (New York: Oxford University Press, 1972), Chapter 5.

In spite of its shortcomings as an instrument of black political power and mobility, the UCD, from the perspective of incumbent authorities, successfully managed black participation at a minimal cost. Tammany's white ethnic leaders (themselves functioning as buffers) created a well-rewarded, compliant black-broker group that organized community political participation, provided organizational support for Tammany candidates, and distributed the relatively meager available white-conferred patronage. The period's militant socialist and nationalist Garveyite movements notwithstanding, Tammany Hall and machines in other large cities with significant black settlements largely succeeded in domesticating black political activity. Notably, the leading instances of racial violence in this period (New York, 1900; Washington and Chicago, 1919) were white initiated; blacks fought and died not in expressive or instrumental protest but in self-defense.

Thus, between 1900 and 1930 the black Northern semicolonies were ruled indirectly through the social-control mechanism of ghetto machine buffers. By contrast, between 1940 and the present, largely as a result of the triumph of reform that shifted the locus of political power in most American cities (Chicago being the most notable exception) from the machines to independent, semiautonomous, but not apolitical bureaucracies, the black ghettos have been administered directly by service bureaucracy personnel, few of whom are black, who have been more responsive to their own standards of conduct than to those they serve and effectively responsible only to themselves. Even the very limited power and autonomy the machines provided blacks in the North were casualties of the reformers' victories. Not surprisingly, most issue-oriented racial conflicts in the past three decades have related directly or obliquely to the control and performance of the bureaucracies, whose impact on the lives of the poor, especially in the absence of party mediation, is overwhelming and alienating.[11] Not surprisingly, too, political and economic elites have used bureaucratic procedures, rewards, and per-

---

[11] For relevant discussions, see Michael Lipsky, *Protest in City Politics* (Chicago: Rand McNally, 1970); and the essays by Michael Rogin, Lewis Lipsitz, Michael Parenti, and Philip Green, in Philip Green and Sanford Levinson (eds.), *Power and Community* (New York: Pantheon, 1969).

sonnel as instruments of social control.[12] Nevertheless, compared to the machines, these mechanisms only do half the job. In currently fashionable policy jargon, machine control dealt with citizen input as well as system output; bureaucratic-control mechanisms, on the other hand, deal only with output. They have taken over the machine's role of distributing benefits and services without assuming the functions of aggregating and transmitting demands.

Thus the ghetto rebellions were symptomatic of, and, in part, caused by, the decay of urban party institutions, which had the capacity to organize broad mass participation into "legitimate" channels. Strong party systems have the capability, in Huntington's words, to "expand participation through the system and thus to preempt or to divert anemic or revolutionary political activity, and second, to moderate and channel the participation of newly mobilized groups in such a manner as not to disrupt the system." Paradoxically, the triumph of urban reform undermined the reformers' presuppositions, interests, and values. And, ironically, the machines' demise has produced a governing dilemma of major proportions for mayors, particularly liberal reform mayors in cities with atrophied party organizations, who typically find they lack sufficient resources to control and direct the autonomous bureaucracies over which they formally preside.[13]

II

The essence of the urban counterrevolution is the attempt by governing executives to create new institutional links to perform the elite-insulating functions of the defunct machines. The counterrevolution's characteristic tool is the repressive reform.

Reform can have many meanings and take many forms. From the perspective of the subordinate, André Gorz has distinguished between two types of reform demands: "reformist" and "non-reformist" or structural reforms. The former "subordinates its objectives to the criteria of rationality and

[12] For a discussion of welfare and social control, see Frances Fox Piven and Richard Cloward, *Regulating the Poor* (New York: Pantheon, 1971).

[13] This is a central theme in Theodore Lowi, *At the Pleasure of the Mayor* (New York: Free Press, 1964).

practicability of a given system and policy." It "rejects those objectives and demands—however deep the need for them— which are incompatible with the preservation of the system." Structural reforms, on the other hand, are "conceived not in terms of what is possible within the framework of a given system and administration, but in view of what should be made possible in terms of human needs and demands." Such reforms assume "a modification of the relations of power . . . a structural reform *always* requires the creation of new centers of domestic power."[14]

Gorz' examples relate to anticapitalist struggles. The choice between reformist and structural demands is a choice between subordinate and autonomous powers:

> By *subordinate* powers must be understood the association or participation by workers in an economic policy which urges them to share the responsibility on the level of results and execution, while at the same time it forbids them to become involved in the decisions and the criteria according to which this policy has been decreed. For example, the union is invited to "participate" in a policy predetermined by others on the company level and to "share" in carrying out this policy. . . .
>
> By *autonomous* power, on the other hand, must be understood the power of workers to challenge, in opposing the effects and methods of implementation, the very premises of the management's policy; to challenge them even in anticipation, because they control all the particulars on the basis of which the management's policy is elaborated.[15]

Thus, structural reforms "modify the relationship of forces," demand "the redistribution of functions and powers, new centers of democratic decision making—aims which prefigure a socialist transformation of society and move towards it."[16] The critical question is thus not simply one of participation, but the structural *terms* of participation. Participation and control are not synonymous.

The most far-reaching instrumental demands by blacks for change in the last half decade have seen demands for control, not just participation; for an end to the structural realities of

[14] André Gorz, *Strategy for Labor: A Radical Proposal* (Boston: Beacon Press, 1967), pp. 7–8.
[15] *Ibid.*, p. 9.
[16] *Ibid.*, p. 58.

internal colonialism, not widened choice possibilities within those parameters; for antonomous power, in short, not subordinate power. By focusing on the police and the schools, blacks demanding community control strike directly at the most consequential agents of social control.

The prerevolutionary combination of mass, black alienation and support for antiproperty, anti-police rebellions and a program of structural, rather than reformist, demands, jolted sophisticated elite members who realized that their interests would be in jeopardy should rebellion become revolution. William Gamson has argued that elites can respond to threatening discontent by either yielding ground ("outcome modification") or "by directing counter-influence, or social control." The social-control response "will generally be preferred to outcome modification since, if it is successful, it will maximize the maneuverability of the recipient of pressure."[17] By utilizing social-control techniques, elites can maintain stability without conceding scarce resources to the discontented. The social-control response is a repressive response.

Liberal political elites have opted for the social-control alternative, but in the guise of outcome modification. To those demanding structural reform, they have offered reformist solutions. But these reformist offerings, we shall see, while appearing to involve structural changes, in fact are boundary-maintaining control mechanisms that utilize the rhetoric of participation, responsiveness, and control. It is this mixture of reformism, which appears to be structural yet seeks to maintain and secure elite dominance in social contexts of potential transformation, that can be labeled repressive reform.

Repression has two meanings: to subdue or put down by force, or, more to the point in this discussion, "to prevent the natural or normal expression, activity, or development of something."[18] The second meaning is akin to Herbert Marcuse's notion of "surplus repression," the set of restrictions necessary to secure the continuity of a particular form of social

---

[17] William A. Gamson, "Stable Unrepresentation in American Society," *American Behavioral Scientist,* 12 (November/December 1968), pp. 18–19.

[18] Elliot Currie, "Repressive Violence," *Transaction* 8 (February 1971), p. 13.

domination.[19] In his classic essay, "The Poor," Simmel drew attention to the conservative and potentially repressive nature of reformism:

> If we take into consideration this meaning of assistance to the poor, it becomes clear that the fact of taking away from the rich to give to the poor does not aim at equalizing their individual positions and is not, even in its orientation, directed at suppressing the social difference between the rich and the poor. On the contrary, assistance is based on the structure of society, whatever it may be; it is in open contradiction to all socialist and communist aspirations which would abolish this social structure. The goal of assistance is precisely to mitigate certain extreme manifestations of social differentiation. If assistance were to be based on the interests of the poor person, there would, in principle, be no limit whatsoever on the transmission of poverty in favor of the poor, a transmission that would lead to the equality of all. But since the focus is the social whole—the political, family, or other socially determined circles—there is no reason to aid the person more than is required by the maintenance of the social *status quo*.[20]

In institutional-political terms, repressive reforms grant participation only to the extent necessary to preserve existing power relationships. The result is inauthentic, formal democracy.[21]

If for the relatively powerless, community control is a decolonizing structural demand, for liberal (repressive) reformers it has assumed a very different meaning. Consider, as a preliminary intellectual example, the work of Alan Altshuler, whose *Community Control: The Black Demand for Participation in Large American Çities* can be read as a handbook for repressive reform. The book, largely directed at white skeptics, takes the form of a brief in favor of "community control." The thrust of the argument is that, sensibly implemented, community control not only does not threaten the existing system, but actually helps insure its preservation:

[19] This concept is developed in Herbert Marcuse, *Eros and Civilization* (Boston: Beacon Press, 1955).

[20] Georg Simmel, "The Poor," in C. I. Waxman (ed.), *Poverty: Power and Politics* (New York: Grosset and Dunlap, 1968), pp. 8–9.

[21] For a discussion, see Amitai Etzioni, *The Active Society* (New York: Free Press, 1968), pp. 633 ff.

I address myself to fellow whites who believe this nation's highest priority must be to achieve a peace of reconciliation. The question for us is more than one of peace; it is one of legitimacy. It is first: how can we sustain the interest of blacks in peaceful compromise—in sharing laws, institutions, even a common nationality with the white majority? And it is second: how can we pursue this aim effectively within the American political system? . . . Here is the crux of the problem. Whites (especially these who live in homogeneous jurisdictions) take the basic values of local government for granted. Blacks do not. Whites disagree on precise spending priorities, and they grouse about tax increases; but they do not question the system itself. Blacks do.[22]

Needed, therefore, are "sources of liaison with the smouldering ghettoes" that can replace "violent disorder with nonviolent political and protest activity," and "establish a form of government that is widely perceived as legitimate in the ghettoes."[23]

Supporting programs that follow the Model Cities precedent (which could hardly be designated examples of meaningful community control), Altshuler argues that "city officials who supported *limited devolutions* of authority to the neighborhood level would be likely to reap a harvest of good will in the black community and (in the case of mayors) of good publicity nationally" (italics added). Of the demands blacks make, he maintains, which include massive income redistribution, better jobs, access to positions of economic and political power, "participatory reform . . . for all the obstacles to it, is probably the most feasible," since most whites "really have no stake in who governs the ghettoes."[24] In this view, reformist community-control concessions by white elites are *substitutes* for other substantive changes.

"The critical issue," Altshuler writes, "is what it will take to persuade blacks that the system is fair." Put another way, the critical issue is stability and elite insulation. Pragmatic doses of community participation will achieve this goal:

[22] Alan A. Altshuler, *Community Control: The Black Demand for Participation in Large American Cities* (New York: Pegasus, 1970), pp. 195, 198.
[23] *Ibid.*, pp. 30, 55.
[24] *Ibid.*, pp. 113, 197.

Perhaps its most important positive potential, from the standpoint of city-wide elected officials, would be to divert much of the force of community dissatisfactions from them to neighborhood leaders. There would still be pressure on the city-wide leaders to find resources for the decentralized functions, but they would be far less vulnerable than currently to blame for day-to-day operations . . . It would provide an arena in which blacks might engage their energies and experience power . . . It would provide a focus for black political organization . . . But most important, it would give blacks a tangible stake in the American political system. By giving them systems they considered their own, it would—hopefully—enhance the legitimacy of the whole system in their eyes.[25]

These elite-sponsored, community-control programs, Altshuler hopes, would domesticate and structure black political participation much as the American labor movement, which concedes subordinate power to workers, domesticates and channels proletarian discontents. "The best resolution of the current racial crisis for which we can hope is that the labor precedent will be emulated."[26]

III

In the past half decade, the institutional development of this program of repressive reform has begun, most notably in Boston and New York. In these cities, reform mayors Kevin White and John Lindsay have created a new class of urban organizations, including neighborhood city halls, urban-action task forces, and pilot programs for neighborhood government, which share the following characteristics:

As distinguished from private pressure groups, at the neighborhood level, these new "linkage" organizations are created by governing executives. Although they are initiated by government, they typically take the form of "mixed" systems (much like the traditional machines), which are neither purely in the private nor purely in the public sector. Typically, too, they are organizations of organizations, bringing together service bureaucracy, mayoral, and voluntary, group repre-

[25] *Ibid.*, pp 203, 112–113, 199.
[26] *Ibid.*, p. 206.

sentatives. In the neighborhoods they serve, these organizations are the officially sanctioned access points to government, the focus of citizen demands. Their assets are tangible; they deliver either services or information about the availability of services. They share the stated or implicit aims of rationalizing and improving municipal services, increasing governmental responsiveness, reducing citizen alienation, and defusing actual or potential conflict. And, most importantly, these organizations structure participation and establish administrative mechanisms for reaching a client neighborhood on elite terms, leaving the existing distribution of political resources and power largely intact.[27]

Consider New York City's neighborhood government program. In June 1970, Mayor Lindsay proposed the establishment of sixty-two "neighborhood government" units, each with a population of approximately 130,000, that would utilize the prevailing boundaries of the city's advisory community-planning boards (appointed by the borough presidents). The program's stated aims might have been drawn up by Altshuler:

> To improve the delivery of municipal services by making city agencies more responsive and accountable at the neighborhood level.
>
> To reduce the distance that citizens feel exists between themselves and city government.
>
> To create the basis for a single coordinated governmental presence in each neighborhood, recognized and supported by the community, the municipal government, and all elected officials.

If implemented fully—to date, six pilot neighborhood governmental programs are functioning—the Lindsay plan would be the most elaborate, and possibly the most emulated, network of linkage organizations in the United States. Accordingly, the origins, aims, structure, and implementation of the plan deserve careful scrutiny.

Neighborhood government is the Lindsay administration's successor to its neighborhood city halls and urban-action task

[27] Many of these characteristics are also shared by the federally initiated Community Action programs and the Model Cities program.

forces, whose powers and functions it assumes. Each neighborhood unit, under the plan, would have an executive community director, appointed by the mayor; and a community board, seven of whose thirteen members would be selected by the mayor, the borough president, and the local councilmen, three by the district school board, and up to three by the poverty corporations and Model Cities boards in the area. Though this precise formula has not been followed in the pilot areas, the mechanisms created do conform to the spirit of the original proposal. In all of the areas the bulk of neighborhood governmental personnel are elite-selected; in none are they chosen directly by the constituency they claim to represent.

The organizational roots of neighborhood government reveal the program's "new machine"[28] character. Running as the Republican-Liberal candidate in 1965, Lindsay lacked even the inadequate organizational support the Democratic party was capable of providing for its candidates. To compensate, his campaign manager organized storefront headquarters in the city's neighborhoods to duplicate the electoral functions of the defunct machines. These storefronts, in spite of Democratic city council opposition, developed into neighborhood city halls, which served as grievance centers that dispensed particularistic rewards. The results of the creation of these new institutional brokers, Lindsay has claimed:

> . . . were almost immediately encouraging. . . . For example, more than 2,300 problems were brought to the city's attention through one neighborhood city hall located in a city-owned health center in Queens. The complaints ran the gamut from housing to street and sewer conditions, from abandoned cars to welfare problems and requests for traffic lights—all the services a city tries to provide for its people. The hall was staffed by three professionals supplemented by volunteers who . . . both as residents and "ombudsmen," . . . could channel complaints and problems directly into the machinery of the city administration.
>
> The results were impressive. The number of cases handled jumped from 2,200 in 1967 to more than 8,000 in the first nine months of 1968. *More important, however, was the fact that local residents realized their neighborhood city hall was an*

[28] Lowi advocated the creation of new machines, *op. cit.*, pp. 215 ff.

effective mechanism for getting grievances resolved [italics added].[29]

Actually, as a 1969 evaluation study carried out for the Mayor's Office of Administration indicated, the city's six neighborhood city halls (these areas later became the locales for the pilot projects in neighborhood government) lacked adequate filing systems, received only sporadic cooperation from the city's bureaucracies, received hardly any help from the program's city-wide coordinators, and relied for results (as did the machines) on personal contacts with friendly bureaucrats. But, as Lindsay indicated, substantive performance counted for far less than mass perceptions of effectiveness.

The urban-action task forces, the second and more important organizational predecessors to neighborhood government, were founded in a conscious effort to cool the ghettos. The problem, as Lindsay saw it, was one of alienation:

> What we saw in early 1966 was that within the ghetto, discontent and alienation were at the breaking point. We saw that a basic commitment to ending that alienation through greater contact was essential. And we knew that words alone would not do the job. . . .
>
>   Thus, throughout the fall of 1966 and into the spring of 1967 we made plans for a structured, formal link between the neighborhoods and the city.[30]

In April 1967, the summer task force was announced, to operate in approximately twenty neighborhoods. A year later, by executive order, the task force was put on a year-round permanent basis to "open channels of communication . . . act as a vehicle for coordinating city services . . . and ensure that the agencies of city government are responsive on a direct basis to neighborhood problems."[31]

Notwithstanding this innocuous statement of intent, the task force institutional network provided City Hall with a potentially potent social-control mechanism, and, secondarily, with the means to begin to assert mayoral control over the

[29] Lindsay, *op. cit.*, p. 118.

[30] *Ibid.*, pp. 87, 95.

[31] City of New York, Executive Order No. 73., April 22, 1968.

bureaucracies. Its most notable feature was organizational dominance by the mayor's office. At the city level, a task force, whose chairman and vice-chairman were appointed by the mayor and whose membership consisted of heads of eighteen city agencies and departments, the borough presidents, and the chairmen of the Board of Education, the Council Against Poverty, and the Housing Authority, supervised the work of the local task forces composed of a mayorally appointed chairman and vice-chairman, neighborhood representatives from the bureaucracies, local elected officials, and "invited community leaders."

Disingenuously, Lindsay has maintained that the task force network might appear to be nothing "but a peacekeeping operation . . . but in fact the task force did more than that," by coordinating services, transmitting grievances, and providing a means of popular participation.[32] The central focus of task force activity, the Kerner Commission more candidly noted, was the prevention of ghetto rebellions; the achievement of this goal depended on the task forces' ability to win community confidence. As in Vietnam, organized service and participatory programs were instruments of pacification:

> The Task Force can make a major contribution to the prevention of civil disorders. If the Task Force has been successful in achieving the objectives stressed above, its members will have gained the confidence of a wide spectrum of ghetto residents. This will enable it to identify potentially explosive conditions, and working with the police, to take action to defuse the situation.[33]

By fusing neighborhood city halls and the task forces, neighborhood government explicitly seeks to duplicate the elite-insulating features of the machines. Whereas traditional liberal reformers fought the machines, their contemporary successors are in the process of creating new ones. But whereas traditional machine politicians did not cloak their particularism with an ideological superstructure, the new reformers try to obscure their aims by co-opting the rhetoric

[32] Lindsay, *op. cit.*, p. 101.

[33] *Report of the National Advisory Commission on Civil Disorders* (New York: Bantam, 1968), p. 290. This report is often referred to as part of the Kerner Commission.

of democratic participation and community control. Everything
is conceded, but nothing changes.

IV

> Institutions, by the very fact of their existence, control human
> conduct by setting up pre-defined patterns of conduct, which
> channel it in one direction as against the many other directions
> that would theoretically be possible. . . . The primary social
> control is given in the existence of an institution as such.[34]

Conversely, the decay of institutions constitutes a breakdown
of patterns of social control. In prerevolutionary (and pre-
counterrevolutionary) America, the breakdown of traditional
institutional patterns of social control is dramatically apparent
in the black community. Indeed, the urban counterrevolution,
led by liberal, repressive reformers, by creating new linkage
organizations in the cities, seeks preeminently to restore
indirect rule to the black semicolonies.

The urban counterrevolution is aimed not only at the semicolonized black population, but at the potentially most disrup-
tive members of the white population as well. As immigrants
and, later, as native born citizens, white ethnic workers have
been linked to the political system through three discrete yet
interacting institutions: the political machines, the Catholic
Church, and the AFL–CIO trade unions. Seen both individually
and as a cluster of social-control mechanisms, each of these
integrating institutions in the past three decades has under-
gone considerable change.[35] As a result, they have lost their
capacity to insure the quiescence and predictability of white-
working-class behavior. Paradoxically, the decay of integrative
white-working-class institutions became pronounced in the
period when liberal elites sought to impose the labor social-
control precedent on American blacks.

The decline of the Democratic party machines has affected
the white ethnics even more directly than blacks. White
Catholic workers controlled the machines; blacks did not. In
the Church, the ecumenism of Pope John, the activities of the

---

[34] Peter Berger and Thomas Luckman, *The Social Construction of Reality*
(Garden City, N.Y.: Doubleday, 1967), p. 55.

[35] These remarks are occasioned by J. David Greenstone's observations in
his unpublished paper, "Ethnicity, Race, and Urban Transformation."

Catholic left, and the closing of many parochial schools have been profoundly unsettling. And, while the party has decayed and the Church has been in ferment, the unions have settled down to a routine economism, activity hardly as exhilarating as the pioneering struggles of the 1930s. By the end of the 1960s, none of the trinity of integrating linkage institutions for the white working class commanded its traditional level of affective solidarity. The machines had become marginal political forces. For many, the Church confused more than it anchored. And the unions—whose relative working-class membership was declining—had become defensive instrumental organizations.

In short, though the levels of political consciousness and overt rebellious behavior for white workers and blacks clearly differed, as for blacks, the traditional elite-insulating, buffer institutions of the white working class had lost most of their effectiveness by the late 1960s. As a result, a high degree of free-floating worker discontent, often ill-understood by the workers themselves, went in search of suitable outlets ranging from sabotage at the work place to support of racist-populist candidates like George Wallace and Mario Proccacino.[36] Gary Wills' description of the audience at a 1968 rally for Spiro Agnew captures the mood and the possibilities:

> They vomit laughter. Trying to eject the vacuum inside them. They are not hungry or underprivileged or deprived in material ways. Each has, in some minor way, "made it." And it all means nothing. Washington does not care. They have worked, and for what? . . . The desire for "law and order" is nothing so simple as a code word for racism; it is a cry, as things begin to break up, for stability, for stopping history in mid-dissolution. Hammer the structure back together; bring nails and bolts and clamps to keep it from collapsing.[37]

Blacks demanding structural change and white workers yearning for an elusive stability share the position of the relatively powerless, who are no longer buffered and separated from elites by social-control mechanisms that work. Both groups are quite obviously discontented; and it is this unstructured discontent that is prerevolutionary.

[36] See Bill Watson, "Counter-Planning on the Shop Floor," *Radical America,* 5 (May/June 1971), 77–85.

[37] Gary Wills, *Nixon Agonistes* (New York: Signet, 1970), pp. 58–59.

From an elite perspective, therefore, it is, at least in the long run, as important to create new linkage institutions for white Catholic workers as it is for the semicolonized blacks. The development of a "white niggers of America"[38] consciousness in the United States might well produce a revolutionary "moment of madness"[39] when, in the absence of traditional restraining social-control mechanisms, the oppressed feel that all is possible. If, for elites, the paramount racial issue is the restoration of a lost legitimacy, the critical working-class issue is the maintenance of a high level of trust threatened by institutional decay.

In this light, the selection of the six pilot areas for New York City's program in neighborhood government makes eminent sense. Brownsville and East New York in Brooklyn, Flushing-Jamaica and Jackson Heights-Corona in Queens, Fordham-Tremont in the Bronx, and Washington Heights-Inwood in Manhattan include some of the city's most desperate ghetto areas and neighborhoods with a high proportion of white ethnic Catholic workers.

Since the development of neighborhood government is most advanced in Washington Heights-Inwood, the process of institutionalization there concretely indicates the potential shape and nature of urban institutions as we move toward 1984. In that racially heterogeneous neighborhood (70 percent white working class, 15 percent black, and 15 percent Puerto Rican), an elaborate participatory mechanism that replicates many of the machine's traditional functions and provides the illusion of meaningful citizen participation in decision making has been established.

Based on Mayor Lindsay's June 1970 plan for neighborhood government, the chairman of the Washington Heights-Inwood urban-action task force (also the First Deputy City Administrator, a Lindsay appointee, and who had been an urban systems analyst for IBM) drew up a pilot program proposing that his neighborhood be one of the program's experimental locales. He argued, two months after the mayor's public state-

[38] Pierre Valliéres, *White Niggers of America* (New York: Monthly Review, 1971).

[39] Aristide Zolberg uses this phrase in his "Moments of Madness: Politics as Art," *Politics and Society,* 2 (February 1972), to explicate the common features of events in Paris during the French Revolution, the Paris Commune, and May 1968.

ment, that Washington Heights was an ideal test site. It was, he noted, an area that was "still relatively stable, but in serious danger of decay," with "enough positive attributes to offer good chance for success." Not only was the area the site of already functioning task force and neighborhood city hall organizations, it also had available to it Neighborhood Action Program (NAP) funds (approximately $500,000 a year) that could be spent at the discretion of the neighborhood government on capital projects requiring little or no continuing maintenance by the city. The advantages of merging the task force, neighborhood city hall, and NAP operations, he suggested, included the development of a single coherent focus for citizen demands, increased possibilities for mayoral control of the performance of the service bureaucracies, and, in the words of his proposal, "NAP money serves as incentive for citizen participation in all aspects of the project." The availability of a relatively inconsequential sum for a neighborhood of 180,000 people would be used to induce local individuals and groups—especially the discontented and alienated—to participate in the new program. The proposal betrayed no concern for municipal liberty, authentic representation, or substantive democracy. Rather, its thrust was the design of a program that at a very low cost could divert the energies of the rebellious into politically harmless system-supportive activity, activity that authorities could cite as evidence of the legitimate, democratic, open responsive nature of the political system. As the proposal made quite clear, the institutionalization of neighborhood government not only was aimed at domesticating and managing participation, but also at creating false consciousness[40] among subordinates who would mistake elite misinterpretations of the efficacy of their participation for an accurate account.

Washington Heights neighborhood government began functioning in the winter 1971. Obviously, only a very preliminary, tentative appraisal of its activity is now possible. Yet it can be noted with assurance that nothing in the organization's experience to date indicates that it is anything but a repressive reform.

[40] Following Isaac Balbus, the case of false consciousness occurs when an individual or group is "affected by" but not "aware of" something. Isaac Balbus, "The Concept of Interest in Pluralist and Marxian Analysis," *Politics and Society,* 1 (February 1971), p. 152.

Mayor Lindsay selected the chairman of the existing advisory community planning board, appointed by the borough president, to be the Executive Director of Washington Heights neighborhood government. After a lengthy series of negotiations between the planning board and representatives of the mayor, mediated by the new director who had close ties with each group, a two-branch "neighborhood government" was created, containing an executive and legislative. Under these arrangements, the executive unit operates in a storefront office, serves as the community's officially sanctioned access point to government, plays the role of "ombudsman" for citizens with grievances against city agencies, and tries to improve the delivery of municipal services in the area and to propose ways to spend the available NAP funds. The planning board acts as the neighborhood's legislature in disposing of the funding proposals. In its first nine months, an elaborate executive structure has been set up that includes, in addition to the office of the director and his permanent staff, fifteen functional committees (parks, safety, health, day care, etc.), with seven to twelve members, who, with few exceptions, have organizational affiliations. These committees conduct hearings at which individuals and groups from the area and service bureaucracy personnel present NAP spending proposals. Those that the committees approve pass on to a "steering committee" of the chairmen of the fifteen functional committees. None of the committee members or chairmen are selected directly or indirectly by mechanisms of community representation. All are chosen by the director. They are accountable to him, and through him to the mayor, not to the community or groups they are said to represent.

The neighborhood legislature—the planning board—depends, in turn, on the political largesse of the borough president. Given their dependency relationships to their political benefactors, the key neighborhood governmental figures are hardly likely to rock the boat. Like traditional machine politicians (they would deny the accuracy of the comparison), they act as brokers between elites and mass; in return for political position and recognition, they insulate elites from challenge both by delivering services and by acting as a lightning rod for conflict and discontent. "We don't have to keep checking with downtown on policy matters, in the director's words, so long as they don't catch flak downtown. That's our job. Flak catchers."[41]

V

The new instruments of linkage and participation now being developed in the cities are instruments of political deception. Under the guise of participatory reformism, they buttress existing oppressive patterns of dominance. In the hands of liberal elites, the early SDS participatory goals, which many of us hoped would substantively democratize America, have been turned on their head.[42] Participation, in these new institutionalized forms, promises to produce only subordinate, not autonomous power as the gap between democratic myth and reality widens. But if, in Gorz' terms, reformist reforms that concede subordinate power are better than none at all, repressive reforms like neighborhood government, even though they may concede subordinate power, are worse than none at all, since they contribute mightily to the process of political mystification.

The quest by the managers of the "urban crisis" to reduce black and white-worker alienation—a goal consciously held and expressed—is, in other terms, an attempt to create false consciousness. The "crisis" is managed not by dealing with objective prerevolutionary patterns of dominance, but by seeking to win trust and to restore legitimacy by appearing to deal with structured power relationships. And, if the literature on the sociology of work is indicative, this strategy, at least in the short run, is likely to succeed. The levels of subjectively perceived worker alienation (feelings of powerlessness, meaninglessness, isolation, and self-estrangement) in the automobile, textile, chemical, and steel industries, Robert Blauner found, varied directly with the perceptions workers held of their control over their work environment. In none of the factory situations examined by Blauner did workers have autonomous control over the factory; in none, too, were they owners, either directly or indirectly through state ownership.

[41] Taken from a personal interview, July 21, 1971.
[42] A good example of this co-option of participation is in F. C. Thayer, "Continuous Democracy," paper presented to the American Political Science Association Meetings, September 1971.

The critical variable accounting for the different levels of discontent was the extent to which the workers were accorded subordinate powers.[43] To define the urban prerevolution as a crisis of legitimacy and alienation is to inquire, of necessity, about the degree of subordinate power that elites should concede to preserve their dominance. To pose the situation in terms of a revolutionary-counterrevolutionary dialectic, on the other hand, requires not only that we choose sides (or at least see that a choice exists) but also that we put the issue in terms of subordinate versus autonomous power, in terms of structural, reformist, and repressive reform.

Should the incipient network of new urban-buffering or broker institutions be developed to organize and manage mass participation, it will be possible to speak accurately of a new "advanced" internal colonialism, characterized by the classic feature of colonial patterns of social control: indirect rule through a broker, native leadership.

Though the precise application of indirect rule has varied in different areas of European and American colonial administration, its essential features have everywhere been the same. Native "chiefs" were integral parts of colonial administration. As the British Governor-General of Nigeria put it in the early years of the century:

> There are not two sets of rulers—British and native—working either separately or in cooperation, but a single government in which the natives have well-defined duties . . . They must be complementary to each other and the chief himself must understand that he has no right to place and power unless he renders his proper services to the state.[44]

In Africa, where traditional chiefs did not exist (for the Kikuyu or the Plateau Tonga of Northern Rhodesia, for example), they were invented.[45] "The colonial administrator turned to them basically because he was faced with the problem of creating an administrative system where none existed." To communi-

---

[43] Robert Blauner, *Alienation and Freedom* (Chicago: University of Chicago Press, 1964).

[44] David Apter, *The Gold Coast in Transition* (Princeton, N.J.: Princeton University Press, 1955), pp. 120–121.

[45] Peter Worsley, *The Third World* (London: Weidenfeld and Nicholson, 1967), p. 38.

cate with and to control the colonized, the colonizers needed authority figures who could provide a "bridge of legitimation" and "enable an administration to divide and rule: popular resentments and hatreds could be deflected onto the local officials while the ultimate authority could remain remote, unseen, and 'above the battle.' "[46] In the essentials, the goals of today's urban counterrevolutionaries are the same.

VI

The new institutional forms discussed in this essay are most appropriate for large, racially and ethnically heterogeneous cities with atrophied party organizations. In other locales, urban counterrevolutionaries have utilized different, yet complementary techniques. The Democratic party machine in Chicago, a curious survivor, continues to link both blacks and white workers to the political system successfully from an elite vantage point. It is not surprising that the overwhelming majority of Chicago businessmen, most of whom are Republicans, enthusiastically support the Daley machine.

In cities with majority or near majority black populations (most notably, Cleveland, Gary, and Newark), black mayors have been elected, usually with the financial support of local and national corporations and foundations. Once in office, irrespective of the degree of their support for fundamental structural change, black mayors typically find it impossible to transform their city's condition. Like those who participate in New York's new linkage organizations, they have subordinate rather than autonomous power with respect to both economic and political elites. In Newark, a community organizer has acutely noted:

> There are 100 men or so, representing the downtown financial centers and suburban political interests, who control land use, planning, and money in this urban colony. . . . Since the decision to "save" Newark, there has been a lot of construction and investment in the downtown area financed by urban renewal money, but . . . with a combination of low corporate taxes, urban renewal tax write-offs, and special tax abatements, the large corporations that build themselves headquarters downtown are building tax sanctuaries that force white property

[46] *Ibid.*

owners to pay back-breaking taxes, force rents up for everyone else and deny the city enough money to maintain even minimal services and schools.[47]

As a result, whether they wish it or not, black mayors often become reluctant brokers, the native "chiefs" in a new system of indirect rule. A former aide to Mayor Kenneth Gibson of Newark has written:

> As blacks and whites grew further apart, the Mayor decided to serve as the conciliator between the two communities as the most sensible thing for him to do. In conflicts of this kind a black mayor must also look beyond the immediate situation. He must maintain harmonious relations with white officials at the city, county, state and federal levels who are in a position to undercut his administration if they do not like his views.[48]

The strategy of black capitalism and corporate penetration of the ghettos, which aims at the creation of a black buffer class of entrepreneurs that owes its position and allegiance to the capitalist system as a whole, complements the political counterrevolution. Of the recent black analyses of prerevolutionary America, Robert Allen's *Black Awakening in White Capitalist America* most centrally grasps this point:

> It is precisely the creation of a new, invigorated black bourgeoisie which is high on corporate America's agenda for the black colony. From the corporate standpoint, such a class would help to stabilize the ghettos, and provide a subtle means of social control. It definitely would not be a revolutionary force . . . Indirect control and manipulation of the black liberation movement was the hallmark of the new liberalism, which even went so far as to endorse black power, and black separatism—not to mention black capitalism—as a means of sidetracking black revolution.[49]

What can be done? Any strategy "must, if it is to succeed, . . . be designed to counter the anticipated response of the

---

[47] Alec Grishkevich, Letter to *The New York Times,* September 7, 1971.

[48] Robert Curvin, "Black Power in Newark: Kenneth Gibson's First Year," paper presented to the American Political Science Association Meetings, September 1971, pp. 8.

[49] Allen, *op. cit.,* pp. 178, 152.

opposition. Any strategy that does not meet this condition—
no matter how militant, nationalist, or revolutionary it may be
—is almost certainly doomed to failure."[50] The identification
and analysis of the developing urban counterrevolution is a
first step in undermining it and in providing the means to
attain the new. Identification and analysis, though, however
precise, are no substitute for action, of course, but unthinking
action will not do either.

A promising strategy for undermining the urban counterrevolution is the Gorzian one of demanding structural, as
opposed to reformist and repressive, reforms, a continuing
process of testing and expanding the limits of the possible.
By virtue of their own stated language and goals, repressive
liberal elites can be overcome:

> Having adopted the rhetoric of democracy in tribute to its own
> ability to manipulate the majority, it is publicly committed to
> the principles of democracy. If its control is weakened, it must
> nevertheless continue to pay lip service to them . . . It is thus
> compelled to wage the battle against democracy covertly—
> forever in danger of being exposed.[51]

In Washington Heights and other "neighborhood government" target areas, opposition groups could begin by demanding that the new governmental unit act as a neighborhood
government in fact as well as form—with autonomous power
to police the police, raise revenue, make all capital spending
and planning decisions for the area, control education, make
bureaucratic appointments, and the like. Confronted with
demands of this order, liberal political elites would have to
choose either to concede them, or to expose their own hollow
rhetoric. Each concession would produce new demands—by
necessity, ultimately, anticapitalist demands—since each
concession would reveal further constraints on the possible.
And each refusal would build consciousness, demystify, and
sharpen the focus of the discontented. Each refusal would be
a powerful tool of political education and organization.

---

[50] *Ibid.*, p. 140.

[51] Benjamin Barber, *Superman and Common Men* (New York: Praeger, 1971),
p. 123.

This strategic position rejects pure reformism, on one hand, and unfocused violence on the other. It offers the possibility of building a democratizing mass revolutionary force. Its aim is to change the direction of the march to 1984 from a numbing movement toward participatory repression to an exhilarating march of liberation. What remains is to do it.

FRANCES FOX PIVEN

an Associate Professor at Columbia University, is one of the founders of the National Welfare Rights Organization, a grass-roots organization of welfare recipients that emerged during the late 1960's. Her written works include *Regulating the Poor* (Random House, 1971), a book analyzing the functions of public welfare, as well as numerous articles on urban politics.

---

the urban crisis: who got what, and why

For quite a while, complaints about the urban fiscal crisis have been droning on, becoming as familiar as complaints about big government, or big bureaucracy, or high taxes—and almost as boring as well. Now suddenly the crisis seems indeed to be upon us: school closings are threatened, library services are curtailed, subway trains go unrepaired, welfare grants are cut, all because big city costs have escalated to the point where local governments can no longer foot the bill. Yet for all the talk, and all the complaints, there has been no convincing explanation of just how it happened that, quite suddenly in the 1960s, the whole municipal housekeeping system seemed to become virtually unmanageable. This is especially odd because, not long ago, the study of city politics and city services was a favorite among American political scientists, and one subject they had gone far to illuminate. Now, with everything knocked askew, they seem to have very little to say that could stand as political analysis.

To be sure, there is a widely accepted explanation. The big cities are said to be in trouble because of the "needs" of blacks for services—a view given authority by the professionals who man the service agencies and echoed by the politicians who depend upon these agencies. Service "needs," the argument goes, have been increasing at a much faster rate than local revenues. The alleged reason is demographic: The large number of impoverished black Southern migrants to the cities presumably requires far greater investments in services, including more elaborate educational programs, more frequent garbage collection, more intensive policing, if the city is to be maintained at accustomed levels of civil decency and order. Thus, city agencies have been forced to expand and elaborate their activities. However, the necessary expansion is presumably constricted for lack of local revenues, particularly since the better off taxpaying residents and businesses have been leaving the city (hastened on their way by the black migration).[1] To this standard explanation of

[1] This view of the urban problem was given official status by the "Riot Commission." According to the commission:

> [The] fourfold dilemma of the American city [is:] Fewer tax dollars come in, as large numbers of middle-income tax payers move out of central cities and property values and business decline; More tax dollars are required, to provide essential public services and facilities, and to meet the needs of expanding lower-income groups; Each tax dollar buys less, because of increasing costs. Citizen dissatisfaction with municipal services grows as needs, expectations and standards of living increase throughout the community [*Report of the National Advisory Commission on Civil Disorders* (New York: Bantam, 1968), p. 389].

Similarly, Alan K. Campbell and Donna E. Shalala write: "Most of the substantive problems flow, at least in part, from . . . the fact that the central cities have been left with segments of the population most in need of expensive services, and the redistribution of economic activities has reduced the relative ability of these areas to support such services" ["Problems Unsolved, Solutions Untried: The Urban Crisis," in *The States and the Urban Crisis* (Englewood Cliffs, N.J.: Prentice-Hall, 1970), p. 7]. The conventional wisdom is again echoed by the U.S. Advisory Commission on Intergovernmental Relations:

> The large central cities are in the throes of a deepening fiscal crisis. On the one hand, they are confronted with the need to satisfy rapidly growing expenditure requirements triggered by the rising number of "high cost" citizens. On the other hand, their tax resources are growing at a decreasing rate (and in some cases actually declining), a reflection of the *exodus of middle and high income families and*

the crisis, there is also a standard remedy: namely, to increase municipal revenues, whether by enlarging federal and state aid to the cities or by redrawing jurisdictional boundaries to recapture suburban taxpayers.[2]

It is true, of course, that black children who receive little in the way of skills or motivation at home may require more effort from the schools; that densely packed slums require more garbage collection; that disorganized neighborhoods require more policing. For instance, the New York City Fire Department reports a 300 percent increase in fires the last twenty years. But fires and similar calamities that threaten a wide public are one thing; welfare, education, and health services, which account for by far the largest portion of big city budgets, quite another. And while by any objective measure the new residents of the city have greater needs for such services, there are several reasons to doubt that the urban crisis is the simple result of rising needs and declining revenues.

For one thing, the trend in service budgets suggests otherwise. Blacks began to pour into the cities in very large numbers after World War II, but costs did not rise precipitously until the mid-1960s.[3] *In other words, the needs of the black*

---

business firms from the central city to suburbia [italics in original] [*Fiscal Balance in the American Federal System: Metropolitan Fiscal Disparities* (Washington, D.C.: Government Printing Office, 1967). Vol. II, p. 5].

Politicians share this view. "In the last 10 years, 200,000 middle-class whites have moved out of St. Louis," said Mayor A. J. Cervantes, "and 100,000 blacks, many of them poor, have moved in. It costs us *eight times as much* to provide city services to the poor as to the middle-class" [italics in original] [*The New York Times,* May 22, 1970].

[2] As a matter of fact, city revenues have not declined at all, but have risen astronomically, although not as astronomically as costs. Presumably if the city had been able to hold or attract better off residents and businesses, revenues would have risen even faster, and the fiscal aspect of the urban crisis would not have developed.

[3] It should be made clear at the outset that the costs of government generally rose steadily in the years after World War II. This is the subject of James O'Connor's analysis in "The Fiscal Crisis of the State," *Socialist Revolution.* 1, 1 (January/February 1970), 12–54; 1, 2 (March/April 1970), 34–94. But while all government budgets expanded, state and local costs rose much faster, and costs in the central cities rose the most rapidly of all, especially after 1965. Thus, according to the Citizen's Budget Commission, New York City's budget increased almost eight times as fast in

poor were not recognized for two decades. For another, any scrutiny of agency budgets shows that, except for public welfare, *the expansion of services to the poor, as such, does not account for a very large proportion of increased expenditures.* It was other groups, *mainly organized provider groups,* who reaped the lion's share of the swollen budgets. The notion that services are being strained to respond to the needs of the new urban poor, in short, takes little account either of when the strains occurred or of the groups who actually benefited from increased expenditures.

These two facts should lead us to look beyond the "rising needs—declining revenues" theory for an explanation of urban troubles. And once we do, perhaps some political common sense can emerge. School administrators and sanitation commissioners may describe their agencies as ruled by professional standards and as shaped by disinterested commitments to the public good, and thus define rising costs as a direct and proper response to the needs of people. But schools and sanitation departments are, after all, agencies of local government, substructures of the local political apparatus, and are managed in response to local political forces. The mere fact that people are poor or that the poor need special services has never led government to respond. Service agencies are political agencies, administered to deal with political problems, not service problems.

Now this view is not especially novel. Indeed, if there is any aspect of the American political system that was persuasively analyzed in the past, it was the political uses of municipal services in promoting allegiance and muting conflict. Public jobs, contracts, and services were dispensed by city bosses to maintain loyal cadres and loyal followers among the heterogeneous groups of the city. Somehow political analysts have forgotten this in their accounts of the contemporary urban crisis, testimony perhaps to the extent to which the doublethink of professional bureaucrats has befogged the common sense of us all. That is, we are confused by changes

---

the five fiscal years between 1964 and 1969 as during the postwar years 1949 to 1954. From an average annual increase of 5.5 percent in 1954, budget costs jumped to 9.1 percent in 1964 and to 14.2 percent in 1969 (*The New York Times,* January 11, 1960). It is with this exceptional rise that this article is concerned.

in the style of urban service politics, failing to see that although the style has changed, the function has not. In the era of the big city machine, municipal authorities managed to maintain a degree of consensus and allegiance among diverse groups by distributing public goods in the form of private favors. Today public goods are distributed through the service bureaucracies. With that change, the process of dispensing public goods has become more formalized, the struggles between groups more public, and the language of city politics more professional. As I will try to explain a little later, these changes were in some ways crucial in the development of what we call the urban crisis. My main point for now, however, is that while we may refer to the schools or the sanitation department as if they are politically neutral, these agencies yield up a whole variety of benefits, and it is by distributing, redistributing, and adapting these payoffs of the city agencies that urban political leaders manage to keep peace and build allegiances among the diverse groups in the city. In other words, the jobs, contracts, perquisites, as well as the actual services of the municipal housekeeping agencies, are just as much the grist of urban politics as they ever were.

All of which is to say that when there is a severe disturbance in the administration and financing of municipal services, the underlying cause is likely to be a fundamental disturbance in political relations. To account for the service "crisis," we should look at the changing relationship between political forces—at rising group conflict and weakening allegiances—and the way in which these disturbances set off an avalanche of new demands. To cope with these strains, political leaders expanded and proliferated the benefits of the city agencies. What I shall argue, in sum, is that the urban crisis is not a crisis of rising needs, but a crisis of rising demands.

Any number of circumstances may disturb existing political relationships, with the result that political leaders are less capable of restraining the demands of various groups. Severe economic dislocations may activate groups that previously asked little of government, as in the 1930s. Or groups may rise in the economic structure, acquiring political force and pressing new demands as a result. Or large scale migrations may alter the balance between groups. Any of these situations may generate sharp antagonism among groups, and, as some new groups acquire a measure of influence, they may undermine established political relationships. In the period of uncertainty that ensues, discontent is likely to spread, political alignments may shift, and allegiances to a political leadership may become insecure. In the context of this general unrest, political leaders, unsure of their footing, are far more likely to respond to the specific demands of specific groups for enlarged benefits or new "rights." Periods of political instability, in other words, nurture new claims and claimants. This is what happened in the cities in the 1960s, and it happened at a time when the urban political system was uniquely ill-equipped to curb the spiral of rising demands that resulted.

The Political Disturbances That Led to Rising Demands

If the service needs of the black poor do not account for the troubles in the cities, the political impact of the black migration probably does. Massive shifts of population are almost always disturbing to a political system, for new relations have to be formed between a political leadership and constituent groups. The migration of large numbers of blacks from the rural South to a few core cities during and after World War II, leading many middle-class white constituents to leave for the suburbs, posed just this challenge to the existing political organization of the cities. But for a long time, local governments resisted responding to the newcomers with the services, symbols, and benefits that might have won the allegiance of these newcomers, just as the allegiance of other groups had previously been won.

The task of political integration was made difficult by at least four circumstances. One was the very magnitude of the influx. Between 1940 and 1960, nearly 4 million blacks left the land and, for the most part, settled in big Northern cities. Consequently, by 1960, at least one in five residents of our fifty largest cities was a black, and in the biggest cities the proportions were much greater. It is no exaggeration to say that the cities were innundated by sheer numbers.

Second, these large numbers were mainly lower-class blacks, whose presence aroused ferocious race and class hatreds, especially among the white ethnics who lived in neighborhoods bordering the ghettos and who felt their homes and schools endangered. As ghetto numbers enlarged, race and class polarities worsened, and political leaders, still firmly tied to the traditional inhabitants of the cities, were in no position to give concessions to the black poor.

Not only was race pitted against race, class against class, but the changing style of urban politics made concessions to conflicting groups a very treacherous matter. Just because the jobs, services, and contracts that fueled the urban political organization were no longer dispensed covertly, in the form of private favors, but rather as matters of public policy, each concession was destined to become a subject of open political conflict. As a result, mayors found it very difficult to finesse their traditional constituents: New public housing for blacks, for example, could not be concealed, and every project threatened to arouse a storm of controversy. Despite their growing numbers and their obvious needs, therefore, blacks got very little in the way of municipal benefits throughout the 1940s and 1950s. Chicago, where the machine style was still entrenched, gave a little more; the Cook County AFDC rolls, for example, rose by 80 percent in the 1950s, and blacks were given some political jobs. But in most cities, the local service agencies resisted the newcomers. In New York City and Los Angeles, for example, the AFDC rolls remained virtually unchanged in the 1950s. In many places public housing was brought to a halt; urban renewal generally became the instrument of black removal; and half the major Southern cities (which also received large numbers of black migrants from rural areas) actually managed to reduce their welfare rolls, often by as much as half.[4]

Finally, when blacks entered the cities, they were confronted by a relatively new development in city politics: namely, the existence of large associations of public employees, whether teachers, policemen, sanitation men, or the like. The provider groups not only had a very large stake in the design and operation of public programs—for there is hardly any aspect of public policy that does not impinge on matters of working conditions, job security, or fringe benefits

[4] For a discussion of the uses of welfare in resisting black migrants, see Frances Fox Piven and Richard A. Cloward, *Regulating the Poor: The Functions of Public Welfare* (New York: Pantheon, 1971), Chapters 7 and 8.

—but they had become numerous enough, organized enough, and independent enough to wield substantial influence in matters affecting their interests.

The development of large, well-organized, and independent provider groups has been going on for many years, probably beginning with the emergence of the civil service merit system at the turn of the century (a development usually credited to the efforts of reformers who sought to improve the quality of municipal services, to eliminate graft, and to dislodge machine leaders).[5] But although the civil service originated in the struggle between party leaders and reformers, it launched municipal employees as an independent force. As city services expanded, the enlarging numbers of public employees began to form associations. Often these originated as benevolent societies, such as New York City's Patrolmen's Benevolent Association, which formed in the 1890s. Protected by the merit system, these associations gradually gained some influence in their own right, and they exerted that influence at both the municipal and the state level to shape legislation and to monitor personnel policies so as to protect and advance their occupational interests.

The result was that, over time, many groups of public employees managed to win substantial control over numerous matters affecting their jobs and their agencies: entrance requirements, tenure guarantees, working conditions, job prerogatives, promotion criteria, retirement benefits. Except where wages were concerned, other groups in the cities rarely became sufficiently aroused to block efforts by public employees to advance their interests. But all of this also meant that when blacks arrived in the cities, local political leaders did not control the jobs—and in cases where job prerogatives had been precisely specified by regulation, did not even control the services—that might have been given as concessions to the black newcomers.

Under the best of circumstances, of course, the task of integrating a new and uprooted rural population into local political structures would have taken time and would have

---

[5] At least some of the employees in all cities with more than 500,000 inhabitants are now under civil service; in about half of these cities, virtually all employees have such protections.

been difficult. But for all of the reasons given, local government was showing little taste for the task. As a result, a large
population that had been set loose from Southern feudal
institutions was not absorbed into the regulating political
institutions (or economic institutions, for they were also
resisted there) of the city. Eventually that dislocated population became volatile, both in the streets and at the polls. And
by 1960, that volatility was beginning to disrupt national
political alignments, forcing the federal government to take
an unprecedented role in urban politics.

By 1960 the swelling urban black population had a key role
in national politics, especially presidential politics. With
migration North, blacks became at least nominal participants
in the electoral system, and their participation was concentrated in the states with the largest number of electoral votes.
By 1960, 90 percent of all Northern blacks were living in the
ten most populous states: California, New York, Pennsylvania,
Ohio, Illinois, New Jersey, Michigan, Massachusetts, Indiana,
and Missouri. It was the heavy Democratic vote in the big
cities of these states, and especially the black Democratic
vote in these cities, that gave Kennedy his slim margin. That
narrow victory helped mark the importance of troubles in the
cities, especially the troubles with blacks in the cities.

Urban blacks, who had been loyal Democrats for almost
three decades, had begun to defect even as their numbers
grew, signaling the failure of the municipal political machinery.
In 1952, 79 percent voted Democratic; by 1956, the black vote
slipped to 61 percent. Kennedy worked to win back some of
these votes (69 percent in 1960) by taking a strong stand on
civil rights in the campaign.[6] But once in office, his administration backed off from supporting civil rights legislation, for
that was sure to jeopardize Southern support. Other ways to
reach and reward the urban black voter were needed.

Accordingly, administration analysts began to explore strategies to cement the allegiance of the urban black vote to the
national party. What emerged, not all at once, but gropingly,
was a series of federal service programs directed to the
ghetto. The first appropriations were small, as with the Juvenile

---

[6] See Piven and Cloward, *op. cit.*, Chapters 9 and 10, on the impact of the
black migration on the Democratic administrations of the 1960s.

Delinquency and Youth Offenses Control Act of 1961, but each program enlarged upon the other, up until the Model Cities legislation of 1966. Some of the new programs—in manpower development, in education, in health—were relatively straightforward. All they did was give new funds to local agencies to be used to provide jobs or services for the poor. Thus, funds appropriated under Title I of the Elementary and Secondary Education Act of 1965 were earmarked for educational facilities for poor children; the medicaid program enacted in 1965 reimbursed health agencies and physicians for treating the poor; and manpower agencies were funded specifically to provide jobs or job training for the poor.

Other of the new federal programs were neither so simple nor so straightforward, and these were the ones that became the hallmark of the Great Society. The federal memoranda describing them were studded with terms like "inner city," "institutional change," and "maximum feasible participation." But if this language was often confusing, the programs themselves ought not to have been. The "inner city," after all, was a euphemism for the ghetto, and activities funded under such titles as delinquency prevention, mental health, antipoverty, or model cities turned out, in the streets of the cities, to look very much alike. What they looked like was nothing less than the old political machine.

Federal funds were used to create new storefront-style agencies in the ghettos, staffed with professionals who helped local people find jobs, obtain welfare, or deal with school officials. Neighborhood leaders were also hired, named community workers, neighborhood aides, or whatever, but in fact close kin to the old ward heelers, for they drew larger numbers of people into the new programs, spreading the federal spoils.

But federal spoils were not enough, for there were not many of them. What the new ghetto agencies had to offer was small and impermanent compared to ongoing municipal programs in education, housing, or health. If blacks were to be wrapped into the political organization of the cities, the traditional agencies of local government, which controlled the bulk of federal, state, and local appropriations, had to be reoriented. Municipal agencies had to be made to respond to blacks.

Various tactics to produce such reform were tried, at first

under the guise of experiments in "institutional change." This meant that the Washington officials who administered the juvenile delinquency program (under Robert Kennedy's direction) required as a condition of granting funds that local governments submit "comprehensive plans" for their own reform (that is, for giving blacks something). But the mere existence of such paper plans did not turn out to be very compelling to the local bureaucrats who implemented programs. Therefore, as turbulence spread in the Northern ghettos, the federal officials began to try another way to promote institutional change—"maximum feasible participation of residents of the areas and members of the groups served." Under that slogan, the Great Society programs gave money to ghetto organizations, which then used the money to harass city agencies. Community workers were hired to badger housing inspectors and to pry loose welfare payments. Lawyers on the federal payroll took municipal agencies to court on behalf of ghetto clients. Later the new programs helped organize the ghetto poor to picket the welfare department or to boycott the school system.

In these various ways, then, the federal government intervened in local politics, and forced local government to do what it had earlier failed to do. Federal dollars and federal authority were used to resuscitate the functions of the political machine, on the one hand *by spurring local service agencies to respond to the black newcomers,* and on the other *by spurring blacks to make demands upon city services.*

As it turned out, blacks made their largest tangible gains from this process through the public welfare system. Total national welfare costs rose from about $4 billion in 1960 to nearly $15 billion in 1970. Big cities that received the largest numbers of black and Spanish-speaking migrants and that were most shaken by the political reverberations of that migration also experienced the largest welfare budget rises. In New York, Los Angeles, and Baltimore, for example, the AFDC rolls quadrupled, and costs rose even faster. In some cities, moreover, welfare costs were absorbing an ever-larger share of the local budget, a bigger piece of the public pie. In New York City, for example, welfare costs absorbed about 12 percent of the city's budget in the 1950s; but by 1970 the share going to welfare had grown to about 25 percent (of a much larger budget), mainly because the proportion of the city's population on Aid to Families of Dependent Children increased from 2.6 percent in 1960 to 11.0 percent in 1970.[7] In other words, the blacks who triggered the disturbances received their biggest payoffs from welfare,[8] mainly because other groups were not competing within the welfare system for a share of relief benefits.[9]

But if blacks got welfare, that was just about all they got. Less obvious than the emergence of black demands—but much more important in accounting for increasing service costs—was the reaction of organized whites to these political developments, particularly the groups who had direct material stakes in the running of the local services. If the new upthrust of black claims threatened and jostled many groups in the city, none were so alert or so shrill as those who had traditionally gotten the main benefits of the municipal services. These were the people who depended, directly or indirectly, on the city treasury for their livelihood: They worked in the municipal agencies, in agencies that were publicly funded (e.g., voluntary hospitals), in professional services that were publicly reimbursed (e.g., doctors), or in businesses that depended on city contracts (e.g., contractors and construction workers). Partly they were incited by black claims that seemed to threaten their traditional preserves. Partly they were no longer held in check by stable relationships with political leaders, for these relations had weakened or become uncer-

[7] Changing Patterns of Prices, Pay, Workers, and Work on the New York Scene, U.S. Department of Labor, Bureau of Labor Statistics (New York: Middle Atlantic Regional Office, May 1971), Regional Reports No. 20, p. 36.
[8] The dole, needless to say, is a very different sort of concession from the higher salaries, pensions, and on-the-job prerogatives won by other groups. For one thing, the dole means continued poverty and low status. For another, it is easier to take away, for recipients remain relatively weak and unorganized.
[9] That poor minorities made large gains through the welfare "crisis" and other groups did not is important to understanding the furious opposition that soaring welfare budgets arouse. Organized welfare-agency workers were competing for the welfare dollar, of course, but were not nearly so successful as the workers in other services, for they were not in a position to take much advantage of political turmoil. They were not nearly so numerous or well organized as teachers, policemen, or firemen, and they could not use the threat of withholding services to exact concessions nearly so effectively. Unlike school teachers or garbage men, their services were of importance only to the very poor.

tain or even turned to enmity: Indeed, in some cases, the leaders themselves had been toppled, shaken loose by the conflict and instability of the times. In effect, the groups who worked for or profited from city government had become unleashed, at the same time that newcomers were snapping at their heels.

The result was that the provider groups reacted with a rush of new demands. And these groups had considerable muscle to back up their claims. Not only were they unusually numerous and well organized, but they were allied to broader constituencies by their class and ethnic ties and by their union affiliations. Moreover, their demands for increased benefits, whether higher salaries or lower work load or greater autonomy, were always couched in terms of protecting the professional standards of the city services, a posture that helped win them broad public support. As a result, even when the organized providers backed up their demands by closing the schools, or stopping the subways, or letting the garbage pile up, many people were ready to blame the inconveniences on political officials.

Local political leaders, their ties to their constituencies undermined by population shifts and spreading discontent, were in a poor position to resist or temper these escalating demands, especially the demands of groups with the power to halt the services on which a broader constituency depended. Instead, to maintain their position, they tried to expand and elaborate the benefits—the payrolls, the contracts, the perquisites, and the services—of the municipal agencies.

Nor, as had been true in the era of the machine, was it easy to use these concessions to restore stable relationships. Where once political leaders had been able to anticipate or allay the claims of various groups, dealing with them one by one, now each concession was public, precipitating rival claims from other groups, each demand ricocheting against the other in an upward spiral. Not only did public concessions excite rivalry, but political officials lost the ability to hold groups in check in another way as well; unlike their machine predecessors, they could attach few conditions to the concessions they made. Each job offered, each wage increase conceded, each job prerogative granted, was now ensconced in civil service regulations or union contracts and, thus firmly secured, could not be withdrawn. Political leaders had lost any leverage in their dealings; each concession simply became the launching pad for higher demands. Instead of regular exchange relationships, open conflict and uncertainty became the rule. The result was a virtual run upon the city treasury by a host of organized groups in the city, each competing with the other for a larger share of municipal benefits. Benefits multiplied and budgets soared—and so did the discontent of various groups with the schools, or police, or housing, or welfare, or health. To illustrate, we need to examine the fiscal impact of mounting political claims in greater detail.

Rising Demands and the Fiscal Crisis

Education is a good example, for it is the single largest service run by localities, accounting for 40 percent of the outlays of state and local government in 1968, up from 30 percent in 1948.[10] The huge expenditures involved in running the schools are also potential benefits—jobs for teachers, contracts for maintenance and construction, and educational services for children—all things to be gained by different groups in the local community. Accordingly, the educational system became a leading target of black demands,[11] at first mainly in the form of the struggle for integrated schools. Later, worn down by local resistance to integration and guided by the Great Society programs that provided staff, meeting rooms, mimeograph

[10] See *State and Local Finances: Significant Features 1967–1970*, U.S. Advisory Commission on Intergovernmental Relations (Washington, D.C.: Government Printing Office, 1969), Figure 6, p. 39.

[11] Conflict and competition over the schools have been further heightened because the proportion of blacks in the schools has increased even more rapidly than the proportion of blacks in the population, owing to the youthfulness of blacks and the flight of whites to private schools. In Washington, blacks constituted 54 percent of the local population in 1965, but 90 percent of the school children; in St. Louis blacks were 27 percent of the population, but 63 percent of the school population; in Chicago, they were 23 percent of the general population, but 53 percent of the school population; in New York City, where blacks and Puerto Ricans make up about 27 percent of the population, 52 percent of the children in the schools were black or Puerto Rican. Of the twenty-eight largest cities in the nation, seventeen had black majorities in the school system by 1965. See *Racial Isolation in the Public Schools,* U.S. Commission on Civil Rights (Washington, D.C.: Government Printing Office, February 20, 1967), Table II–2.

machines, and lawyers to ghetto groups,[12] the difficult demands
for integration were transformed into demands for "citizen
participation," which meant a share of the jobs, contracts, and
status positions that the school system yields up.[13]

Blacks made some gains. Boards of education began hiring
more black teachers, and some cities instituted schemes for
"community control" that ensconced local black leaders in
the lower echelons of the school hierarchy.[14] But the organized
producer groups, whose salaries account for an estimated 80
percent of rising school costs,[15] made far larger gains. Incited
by black claims that seemed to challenge their traditional
preserves and emboldened by a weak and conciliatory city
government, the groups who depend on school budgets began
rapidly to enlarge and entrench their stakes. Most evident in
the scramble were teaching and supervisory personnel, who
were numerous and well organized and became ever more
strident—so much so that the opening of each school year
is now signaled by news of teacher strikes in cities through-

---

[12] The federal government was also providing direct funds to improve the
education of the "disadvantaged" under Title I of the Elementary and
Secondary Education Act of 1965. However, although in four years following the passage of the Act, \$4.3 billion was appropriated for Title I, it was
widely charged that these funds were misused and diverted from the poor
by many local school boards.

[13] A series of training guides to such efforts, prepared with federal funds by
a local poverty program known as United Bronx Parents, included a kit on
"How to Evaluate Your School" and a series of leaflets on such matters as
"The Expense Budget—Where Does All the Money Go?" "The Construction Budget—When the Community Controls Construction We Will Have
the Schools We Need," as well as an all-purpose handbook on parents
rights vis-à-vis the schools. Not surprisingly, Albert Shanker, president of
the teachers union in New York City, charged there was "an organized
effort to bring about rule in the schools by violence," involving the use of
flying squads of disrupters who went from school to school and who, he
said, had been trained with government (i.e., poverty program) funds (*The
New York Times,* November 16, 1970, p. 2).

[14] See Urban America, Inc., and the Urban Coalition, *One Year Later: An
Assessment of the Nation's Response to the Crisis Described by the
National Advisory Commission on Civil Disorders* (New York: Praeger,
1969), pp. 34–35. See also, Naomi Levine with Richard Cohen, *Oceanhill-
Brownsville: A Case History of Schools in Crisis* (New York: Popular
Library, 1969), pp. 127–128.

[15] This estimate was reported by Fred Hechinger, *The New York Times,*
August 29, 1971.

out the country. And threatened city officials strained to
respond by expanding the salaries, jobs, programs, and privileges they had to offer. One result was that average salaries
in New York City, Chicago, Los Angeles, Philadelphia, Washington, D.C., and San Francisco topped the $10,000 mark by
1969, *in most instances having doubled* in the decade. Nationally, teachers' salaries have risen about 8 percent each year
since 1965.[16] Not only did the teachers win rapid increases in
salaries but, often prompted by new black demands, they
exploited contract negotiations and intensive lobbying to win
new guarantees of job security, increased pensions, and "improvements" in educational policy that have had the effect of
increasing their own ranks—all of which drove up school
budgets, especially in the big cities where blacks were concentrated.[17] In Baltimore, where the black population has
reached 47 percent, the school budget increased from $57
million in 1961 to $184 million in 1971; in New Orleans from
$28.5 million to $73.9 million in 1971; in Boston, school costs
rose from $35.4 million in 1961 to $95.7 million in 1971.[18] Total
national educational costs, which in 1957 amounted to $12 bil-
lion, topped $40 billion by 1968,[19] and the U.S. Office of Educa-

[16] Averaging $9,200 in 1970–1971, according to the National Education
Association.

[17] State averages reflect the political troubles in big cities. Thus, in an
urban state like New York, $1,251 was spent per pupil in 1969–1970 and
New Jersey, California, Connecticut, and Massachusetts were not far
behind. This represented an increase of about 80 percent in per pupil
expenditures since 1965–1966.

[18] Educational costs have also risen sharply outside the central cities,
particularly in the adjacent suburban school districts. These rises are a
direct reverberation of troubles in the cities. Suburban school boards
must remain competitive with the rising salary levels of educational personnel in the central cities, particularly considering the high priority placed
on education by the middle-class suburbs. For example, between 1968 and
1969, enrollment in the Westchester, New York, schools increased by 1.5
percent, and the operating budget by 12 percent. In Fairfield, Connecticut,
enrollment increased by 5.2 percent, the budget by 13.2 percent. In Suffolk
County, New York, enrollment increased by 6.6 percent, the budget by 11.6
percent. In Monmouth, New Jersey, enrollment increased by 4.4 percent,
the budget by 19 percent. Moreover, there are also increasing numbers of
blacks in some of the older suburbs, with the result that these towns are
experiencing political disturbances very similar to those of the big cities.

[19] *State and Local Finances, op. cit.,* p. 39.

tion expects costs to continue to rise, by at least 37 percent by 1975. In this process, blacks may have triggered the flood of new demands on the schools, but organized whites turned out to be the main beneficiaries.

What happened in education happened in other services as well. Costs rose precipitously across the board as mayors tried to extend the benefits of the service agencies to quiet the discordant and clamoring groups in the city. One way was to expand the number of jobs, often by creating new agencies, so that there was more to go around. Hence, in New York City, the municipal payroll expanded by over 145,000 jobs in the 1960s, and the rate of increase doubled after Mayor John V. Lindsay took office in 1965.[20] By 1971, 381,000 people were on the municipal payroll. Some 34,000 of these new employees were black and Puerto Rican "paraprofessionals," according to the city's personnel director. Others were Lindsay supporters, put on the payroll as part of his effort to build a new political organization out of the turmoil.[21] Most of the rest were new teachers, policemen, and social workers, some hired to compensate for reduced work loads won by existing employees (teachers won reduced class sizes, patrolmen the right to work in pairs), others hired to staff an actual expansion that had taken place in some services to appease claimant groups who were demanding more welfare, safer streets, or better snow removal.[22] As a result, total state and local governmental employment in the city rose from 8.2 percent of the total labor force in 1960 to 14 percent in 1970. A similar trend of expanded public employment took place in other big cities. In Detroit state and local employment rose from 9 percent of the labor force in 1960 to 12.2 percent in 1970; in Philadelphia from 6.9 percent to 9.8 percent; in Los Angeles

[20] *Changing Patterns of Prices, Pay, Workers, and Work, op. cit.,* pp. 7–8.

[21] Some 25,000 of the new jobs were noncompetitive (*The New York Times,* May 28, 1971). Not surprisingly, the governor suggested that the mayor economize by cutting these, instead of always talking about cutting the number of policemen and firemen.

[22] Welfare is the main example of an actual expansion of services, for the number of welfare employees increased largely as a reflection of increasing caseloads. But so were new policemen hired to appease a broad constituency concerned about rising crime, sanitation men to answer demands for cleaner streets, and so forth.

from 9.8 percent to 12.0 percent; in San Francisco, from 12.2 percent in 1960 to 15.2 percent in 1970.[23]

Another way to try to deal with the clamor was to concede larger and larger salaries and more liberal pensions to existing employees who were pressing new demands, and pressing hard, with transit, or garbage, or police strikes (or sick-outs or slowdowns) that paralyzed whole cities.[24] In Detroit, garbage collectors allowed refuse to accumulate in the streets when the city offered them only a 6 percent wage increase, after the police won an 11 percent increase.[25] In Cincinnati, municipal laborers and garbage collectors threatened a "massive civil disobedience campaign" when they were offered less than the $945 annual raise won by policemen and firemen.[26] In Philadelphia garbage collectors engaged in a slowdown when a policeman was appointed to head their department.[27] A San Francisco strike by 7,500 city workers shut down the

---

[23] Changing Patterns of Prices, Pay, Workers, and Work, op. cit., p. 9. Moreover, big payrolls were a big city phenomenon. A study showed that, in three states studied in detail, the ratio of public employment per 100 population varied sharply by city size, more so in New Jersey and Ohio, less markedly in Texas. See Urban and Rural America: Policies for Future Growth, U.S. Advisory Commission on Intergovernmental Relations (Washington, D.C.: Government Printing Office, April 1968), pp. 47–49.

[24] According to Harold Rubin:

Time lost by state and local government employees due to work stoppages climbed from 7,510 man-days in 1958 to 2,535,000 man-days in 1968, according to the U.S. Bureau of Labor Statistics. Such strikes have not been limited to those performing "nonessential duties." For example, during the first half of 1970 there have been strikes by prison guards (New Jersey), sanitation men (Cincinnati, Ohio; Phoenix, Arizona; Atlanta, Georgia; Seattle, Washington; and Charlotte, North Carolina), teachers (Youngstown, Ohio; Minneapolis, Minnesota; Butte, Montana; Tulsa, Oklahoma; Boston, Massachusetts; Newark and Jersey City, New Jersey; and Los Angeles, California, to list only some of the larger school systems involved), bus drivers (Cleveland, Ohio; Tacoma, Washington; and San Diego, California), hospital employees (State of New Jersey; Detroit, Michigan), policemen (Newport, Kentucky; Livonia, Michigan; and Winthrop, Massachusetts), and firemen (Newark, Ohio, and Racine, Wisconsin) ["Labor Relations in State and Local Governments," in Robert A. Connery and William V. Farr (eds.), Unionization of Municipal Employees (New York: Columbia University, The Academy of Political Science, 1971), pp. 20–21.

[25] The New York Times, June 13, 1971.

[26] The New York Times, January 31, 1970.

[27] The New York Times, February 26, 1970.

schools and the transit system and disrupted several other
services simultaneously.[28] An unprecedented wildcat strike
by New York City's policemen, already the highest paid police
force in the world, would have cost the city an estimated
$56,936 a year for every policeman (and $56,214 for every
fireman), if demands for salaries, pensions, fringe benefits,
and reduced work time had been conceded.[29] If these demands
were perhaps a bit theatrical, the pay raises for city employees
in New York City did average 12 percent each year in 1967,
1968, and 1969. Meanwhile, the U.S. Bureau of Labor Statistics
reported that the earnings of health professionals in the city
rose by 80 percent in the decade, at least double the increase
in factory wages. In other cities across the country similar
groups were making similar gains; municipal salaries rose by
7–10 percent in both 1968 and 1969, or about twice as fast as
the Consumer Price Index.[30]

The pattern of crazily rising municipal budgets is the direct
result of these diverse and pyramiding claims on city services,
claims triggered by political instability.[31] Accordingly, budget

---

[28] *The New York Times,* March 17, 1970.

[29] *The New York Times,* March 15, 1971. These estimates were given to the
press by the city's Budget Director.

[30] Rising wages and pensions benefits among municipal employees are
frequently attributed to unionization, which has indeed spread in the 1960s,
rather than to changes in city politics. Membership in the American Federation of State, County, and Municipal employees increased from 180,000
to 425,000 in one decade; The American Federation of Teachers enlarged
its ranks from 60,000 members in 1961 to 175,000 in 1969. But to point to
unionization as a cause simply diverts the argument, since the spread and
militancy of unionism among city employees in the 1960s must itself be
explained. In any case, a Brookings Institution study of nineteen local
governments showed no conclusive differences between unionized and
nonunionized wages; both had risen substantially. See David Stanley, "The
Effect of Unions on Local Governments," Connery and Farr (eds.), *op. cit.,*
p. 47.

[31] Norton Long and others have argued that the city's economic problems
are largely the result of efforts by city employees to keep up with pay
scales in the private sector, despite the absence of productivity increases
in public service jobs comparable to those that justify wage increases in
the private sector, "The City as Reservation," *The Public Interest,* No. 25
(Fall 1971). This argument, however, presumes that city pay scales lag
behind private scales and that city workers are merely straining to catch
up. Quite the opposite has come to be true in some big cities. A 1970
study by the Middle Atlantic Bureau of Labor Statistics of pay rates in the

trends followed political trends. New York City, for example, received about 1.25 million blacks and Puerto Ricans in the years between 1950 and 1965, while about 1.5 million whites left the city. The political reverberations of these shifts weakened the Democratic party organization and resulted in the Lindsay victory on a fusion ticket in 1965. But the Lindsay government was extremely unstable, without ties to established constituents, virtually without a political organization, and extremely vulnerable to the demands of the different groups, including the ghetto groups whose support it was trying to cultivate. New York also had very strong and staunch provider groups, as everyone knows from the transit, garbage, teacher, and police strikes, each of which in turn threatened municipal calamity. The subsequent escalation of demands by blacks and Puerto Ricans on the one hand, and municipal provider groups on the other, produced the much publicized turmoil and conflict that racked the city.

To deal with these troubles, city officials made concessions, with the result that the municipal budget almost quadrupled in the last decade. And as the turmoil rose, so did city costs: an annual budget rise of 6 percent in the 1950s and 8.5 percent in the early 1960s became an annual rise of 15 percent after 1965.[32] New York now spends half again as much per capita

---

New York metropolitan area found city pay rates to be much higher than private industry rates. For example, carpenters, electricians, and plumbers who worked for the city earned fully 60 percent more than those in private industry; painters and automobile mechanics earned 36 percent more; even messengers, typists, switchboard operators, and janitors were substantially better off when they worked for the city. Moreover, *city workers also received far better holiday, vacation, health insurance, and pension benefits.* It should also be noted that all but the last grouping were also much better paid in the city than in the suburbs. And so were patrolmen, firemen sanitation men, and social workers substantially better paid in the city than in the suburbs. A similar conclusion was reached by Bennett Harrison, who compared mean weekly earnings in the public and private sector of twelve metropolitan areas, using 1966 data. His calculations reveal a sharp disparity between public and private earnings in the central cities (although in 1966 some categories of suburban earnings were higher than the central city). See his *Public Employment and Urban Poverty* (Washington, D.C.: The Urban Institute, 1971), p. 30.

[32] Put another way, the average annual increase in New York City's expense budget during the last five years was $582 million, or eight times as high as the $71 million annual average increase from fiscal 1949 to fiscal 1954.

as other cities over a million (excluding educational costs), twice as much per capita as cities between 500 thousand and a million, and three times as much as the other 288 cities.[33]

A few cities where the existing political organization was firmly entrenched and machine-style politics still strong were spared. Chicago is the notable example, and Chicago's political organization shows in lower welfare costs, in per pupil expenditures that are half that of New York City, in garbage collection costs of $22 a ton compared to $49 in New York City. Mayor Daley never lost his grip. With the white wards firmly in tow, he made modest concessions to blacks earlier and without fear of setting off a chain reaction of demands by other groups. And so he never gave as much, either to blacks or to organized whites. But most other large cities show a pattern of escalating discontent and escalating service budgets more like New York City than Chicago.[34] By 1970, the total

[33] Report on Financing Our Urban Needs," *Our Nation's Cities* (Washington, D.C.: Government Printing Office, March 1969), p. 21.

[34] According to *Fiscal Balance in the American Federal System:*

National aggregates for 1957 and 1962 and more restricted data for 1964–65 indicate that local government in the metropolitan areas spends more and taxes more per person than in the remainder of the country . . . there is a striking contrast in non-educational expenditures —which include all the public welfare, health, hospital, public safety and other public services essential to the well-being of citizens. These general government costs are two-thirds higher in the metropolitan areas than they are in the rest of the country" [*op. cit.,* Vol. II, p. 59].

Specifically, per capita expenditures during 1964–1965 averaged $301.20 in the thirty-seven largest metropolitan areas, compared to $218.31 in small or nonmetropolitan areas (*ibid.,* Table 16, p. 60). As for the central cities themselves, "central cities contained 18.6 percent of the population (in 1964–65), but accounted for almost 25 percent of all local expenditure." In per capita terms, local government expenditure in the large central cities "was 21 percent higher than in their outside regions, and almost two-thirds above that for the rest of the nation" (*ibid.,* p. 62). Moreover, when educational costs are omitted (suburban communities spend a great deal on education), the thirty-seven largest central cities "had an outlay of $232 per capita in 1965—$100 greater than their suburban counterparts" (*ibid.,* p. 6). By 1966–1967, the disparity had become more dramatic in many cities. Per capita general expenditures, *including* education costs, was $475 in Washington, D.C., compared to $224 in the Washington suburban ring; $324 in Baltimore, compared to $210 in the suburban ring; $441 in Newark, compared to $271 in the suburban ring; $335 in Boston, compared to $224 in the suburban ring; $267 in St. Louis, and $187 in the suburbs (*State and Local Finances, op. cit.,* p. 70). Similarly, a study

costs of local government had risen about 350 percent over 1950.

The cities are unable to raise revenues commensurate with these expenditures; and they are unable to resist the claims that underlie rising expenditures. And that is what the fiscal crisis is all about. Cities exist only by state decree, and depend entirely on the state governments for their taxing powers.[35] Concretely this has meant that the states have taken for themselves the preferred taxes[36] leaving the localities to depend primarily on the property tax (which accounts for 70 percent of revenues raised by local governments),[37] supplemented by a local sales tax in many places, user charges (e.g., sewer and water fees), and, in some places, a local income tax.[38] The big cities have had little choice but to drive

---

of fifty-five local governments in the San Francisco-Oakland metropolitan area showed that both the property tax rate and the level of per capita expenditures were higher in the central city. In dormitory suburbs, per capita expenditures were only 58 percent of those in the central city. See Julius Margolis, "Municipal Fiscal Structure in a Metropolitan Region," *Journal of Political Economy*, 65 (June 1957), p. 232.

[35] The New York State Constitution, for example, specifies that:

It shall be the duty of the Legislature, subject to the provisions of this Constitution, to restrict the power of taxation, assessment, borrowing money, contracting indebtedness, and loaning the credit of counties, cities, towns and villages, so as to prevent abuses in taxation and assessments and in contracting of indebtedness by them. Nothing in this article shall be construed to prevent the Legislature from further restricting the powers herein specified [Article VIII, Section 12].

Traditionally the states have granted powers of taxation to the localities only very reluctantly.

[36] Not only do states limit the taxing powers of localities, but they have the authority to mandate local expenditures—e.g., salary increases for police and firemen—with or without adjusting local taxing powers to pay for them. They also have the authority to vote tax exemptions at local expense for favored groups. State legislatures are given to doing exactly that, exacerbating the financial plight of local governments.

[37] This was $27 billion out of $40 billion that localities raised in revenues from their own sources in 1967–1968 *(State and Local Finances, op. cit.,* Table 8, p. 31). It should be noted that property taxes are declining relative to other sources of local revenue. At the turn of the century about 80 percent of state and local budgets were financed by the property tax. Today, the states hardly rely on it at all. Nevertheless, local governments still finance about half their budgets with property taxes.

[38] The first city income tax was levied in Philadelphia, in 1939, when the city was on the verge of bankruptcy. The use of the income tax by big

up these local taxes to which they are limited, but at serious costs.[39] New York City, for example, taxes property at rates twice the national average, yielding a property tax roll three times as large as any other city. New York City also has an income tax, which is rising rapidly. Newark, plagued by racial conflict, ranks second in the nation in its rate of property tax.[40]

The exploitation of any of these taxes is fraught with dilemmas for localities. By raising either property or sale taxes excessively, they risk driving out the business and industry on which their tax rolls eventually depend, and risk also the political ire of their constituents. For instance, it was estimated that a 1 percent increase in the New York City sales tax had the effect of driving 6 percent of all clothing and household furnishing sales out beyond the city line, along with thousands of jobs.[41] A New York property tax rate of 4 percent of true value on new improvements is thought by many to have acted as a brake on most new construction, excepting the very high yielding office buildings and luxury apartments. Boston's 6 percent of true value property tax brought private construction to a halt until the law was changed so that new improvements were taxed only half as heavily as existing buildings.[42]

---

cities spread in the 1960s, with Akron and Detroit adopting it in 1962, Kansas City in 1964, Baltimore and New York City in 1966, and Cleveland in 1967. See *City Income Taxes* (New York: Tax Foundation, Inc., 1967), Research Publication No. 12, pp. 7–9. City income taxes must, of course, also be approved by the state, an approval that is not always forthcoming.

[39] By 1964–1965, per capita local taxes in the central cities of the thirty-seven largest metropolitan areas had risen to $200 per capita. In Washington, D.C., taxes were $291 per capita; in New York City $279; and in Newark $273. Overall, central city residents were paying 7 percent of their income in local taxes and in the biggest cities 10 percent (*Fiscal Balance in the American Federal System, op. cit.*, Vol. II, pp. 75–79).

[40] By 1968, official statistics for the nation as a whole showed local property taxes totaling $27.8 billion. The annual rise since then is estimated at between $1 and $3 billion.

[41] *Our Nation's Cities, op. cit.*, p. 24.

[42] *Our Nation's Cities, op. cit.*, pp. 36–37. To understand the full impact of property taxes, one must remember that these are taxes on capital value, and not on income yielded. Thus, a 3 percent of true value tax on improvements can easily tax away 75 percent of the net income that a new building would otherwise earn—a loss, economists generally agree, that tends to be passed on to consumers. See, for example, Dick Netzer, Economics of the Property Tax (Washington, D.C.: The Brookings Institute, 1966), pp. 40–62.

Increases in either sales or property tax rates thus entail the serious danger of diminishing revenues by eroding the tax base. To make matters worse, with the beginning of recession in 1969, revenues from sales and income taxes began to fall off, while the interest the cities had to pay for borrowing rose, at a time that local governments were going more and more into hock.[43]

Fiscal Constraints and Political Turmoil

In the face of fiscal constraints, demands on city halls do not simply stop. Indeed, a number of frustrated claimants seem ready for rebellion. When pension concessions to some employees in New York City were thwarted by the state legislature, the enraged municipal unions closed the bridges to the city and allowed untreated sewage to flow into the city's waterways, while the president of Local 237 intoned that "Governor Rockefeller needs to be reminded that the teamsters are made of sterner stuff than the people of Czechoslovakia and Austria who caved in so easily to Hitler three decades ago."[44] If most groups were less dramatic in pressing their demands, it is probably because they were more quickly conciliated than these workers, many of whom were black and Puerto Rican. The political instability, which escalating

[43] Local tax collections increased by 500 percent between World War II and 1967, but costs have risen 10 percent faster, and the bigger the city, the tighter the squeeze. If the process were to continue, and today's growth rate of city spending vs. city revenues to continue, a recent study commissioned by the National League of Cities estimates a gap of $262 billion by 1980 (*Our Nation's Cities, op. cit.,* p. 22). Measured another way, state and local indebtedness combined rose by 400 percent since 1948, while the federal debt rose by only 26 percent (*U.S. Fiscal Balance in the American Federal System, op. cit.,* Vol. I, p. 55). In the thirty-six large central cities alone, the cumulative tax gap could reach $25 to $30 billion by 1975 (*Ibid.,* Vol. II, p. 91). A special Commission on the Cities in the Seventies, established by the National Urban Coalition, concluded that by 1980 most cities will be "totally bankrupt" (*The New York Times,* September 24, 1971).

[44] The statement went on to say "that which is good enough for white cops and firemen is good enough for black and Puerto Rican employees of New York City" (*The New York Times,* June 8, 1971). According to city officials, the annual cost of pension benefits, which had been $215 million in 1960, was projected to reach $1.3 billion in the next ten years (*The New York Times,* June 9, 1971).

demands both signify and exacerbate, rocked one city government after another. Indeed, many big city mayors simply
quit the job, something that does not happen very often in
politics.

The reason they give is money—money to appease the
anarchic demands of urban groups. Joseph Barr, former Mayor
of Pittsburgh and a past president of the United States Conference of Mayors, explained that "the main problem of any
mayor of any city of any size is money . . . we are just choked
by the taxes. The middle classes are fleeing to the suburbs
and the tax base is going down and down . . . if the mayors
don't get relief from the legislatures, God help them! . . . Any
mayor who is not frustrated is not thinking." Arthur Naftalin,
former Mayor of Minneapolis and also a past president of the
United States Conference of Mayors, said that the "most difficult and most important problem [is that the city] can't
reach the resources. The states have kept the cities on a
leash, tying them to the property tax—which is regressive.
Old people and low-income people live in the city, and they
catch the burden increasingly." Thomas C. Tarrington, Mayor
of Denver 1963–1968—when he resigned in midterm, said when
he left:

> I hope to heaven the cities are not ungovernable . . . [but] with
> perhaps few if any exceptions, the financial and organizational
> structures of most large cities are hardly up to the needs of
> 1969 or 1970. Our cities were structured financially when we
> were a rural nation and our structures of government are such
> that the mayors lack not only the financial resources but the
> authority to do the job.

Ivan Allen, Jr., Mayor of Atlanta since 1962: "At my age I
question whether I would have been physically able to continue for another four years in the face of the constant pressure, the innumerable crises, and the confrontations that have
occurred in the cities." A. D. Sillingson, Mayor of Omaha from
1965: "I've gone through three and a half tough years in this
racial business, and I could just stand so much." And the
country's first black mayor, Carl B. Stokes of Cleveland, inter-
viewed before he was reelected by the slimmest of margins
in 1969, announced that the biggest challenge facing someone
in his position was "obtaining the necessary money with which

to meet the necessary needs of a big city."[45] Mr. Stokes declined to run again in 1971, leaving Cleveland politics fragmented among eleven different candidates. The list of prominent mayors who threw in the sponge includes such celebrated urban reformers as Jerome P. Cavanaugh of Detroit and Richard C. Lee of New Haven. Nearly half the United States Conference of Mayors Executive Committee and Advisory Council have retired or announced their intentions of retiring after their present term, an "unprecedented" number according to a Conference spokesman.

Whether the candidates were new aspirants moving in to fill the vacuum or older hands sticking it out, by 1969 big city elections throughout the country reflected the instability of the times. Mayor Lindsay was reelected, but with only 42 percent of the vote. The same year two Democrats ran against each other in Detroit. In Pittsburgh Peter F. Flaherty, an insurgent Democrat, won only to promptly repudiate the ward chairman who turned out the vote for him; in Youngstown, a solidly Democratic city, a Republican was elected; in Philadelphia, where registration is heavily Democratic, the Democratic party was unable to block a Republican sweep headed by District Attorney Arlen Specter, putting him in line for a try at the Mayor's office. Of 156 Connecticut towns and cities that held elections in 1969, 46 municipalities switched parties. And an assembly of eight-five representatives of federal, state, and local governments, labor and religious leaders, editors and educators, meeting at Arden House in 1969, pronounced:

> America is in the midst of an urban crisis demonstrating an inadequacy and incompetency of basic policies, programs and institutions and presenting a crisis of confidence. These failures affect every public service—education, housing, welfare, health, and hospitals, transportation, pollution control, the administration of criminal justice, and a host of others—producing daily deterioration in the quality of life. Although most visible in the large cities, that deterioration spreads to suburbia, exurbia, and beyond. Frustration rises as government fails to respond.[46]

This pronouncement came not from a radical caucus, but from

[45] The Christian Science Monitor, September 4, 1969.
[46] The States and the Urban Crisis, Report of the Thirty-Sixth American Assembly (Harriman, N.Y.: Arden House, October 30–November 2, 1969). The Report went on, not surprisingly, to recommend increased state and federal aid for the cities.

a gathering of the most prestigious representatives of American institutions.

Those who for the time survived the turmoil were even shriller in sounding the alarm. Mayor Joseph Alioto of San Francisco said simply: "The sky's falling in on the cities; it really is. We've had six cops killed in San Francisco since I took office. We need jobs and money for the poor and haven't money for either . . . We can't go on like this. Even the capitalistic system's not going to survive the way we're going." Kenneth Gibson, the black Mayor of Newark: "Wherever the cities are going, Newark's going to get there first . . . If we had a bubonic plague in Newark everybody would try to help, but we really have a worse plague and nobody notices." Mayor Wesley Uhlman of Seattle said he was so busy putting out fires, he had no time to think about anything else. Moon Candrieu, the Mayor of New Orleans: "We've taxed everything that moves and everything that stands still, and if anything moves again, we tax that too . . . The cities are going down the pipe and if we're going to save them we'd better do it now; three years from now will be too late." "Boston," said Mayor Kevin White, "is a tinderbox . . . The fact is, it's an armed camp. One out of every five people in Boston is on welfare. Look, we raise 70 percent of our money with the property tax, but half our property is untaxable and 20 percent of our people are bankrupt. Could you run a business that way?" And Mayor Lindsay of New York proclaimed: "The cities of America are in a battle for survival . . . Frankly, even with help in Washington, I'm not sure we can pull out of the urban crisis in time."[47] (Not long afterwards, Governor Rockefeller suggested that perhaps New York City's government, at least, ought not to survive, that it might be a good idea to abolish the present city structure, and begin all over).[48]

[47] James Reston, "The President and the Mayors," *The New York Times*, March 24, 1971. In another column on April 21, 1971, Reston summarized the reports of the big city mayors as: "First, they felt the crisis of the cities was the major threat to the security of the nation—more serious than Vietnam or anything else. Second, they felt that the bankruptcy and anarchy were underestimated. . . . They sound like communiques from a battlefield. . . . They have got beyond all the questions of race or party and are looking for power and leadership to deal with the urban problem."
[48] The Governor said he had in mind a new structure like the London County Council. City political leaders, for their part, had been proposing to abolish city-state relations by declaring New York City a separate state.

The mayors speak of the twin troubles of scarce revenues and racial confrontation. And it is no accident that the troubles occur together and are most severe in the biggest cities. It was the biggest cities that experienced the most serious disturbance of traditional political relations as a result of the influx of blacks and the outflux of many whites. In this context, demands by black newcomers triggered a rush of new demands by whites, especially the large and well-organized provider groups that flourished in the big cities. The weakened and vulnerable mayors responded; they gave more and more of the jobs, salaries, contracts, and services that had always worked to win and hold the allegiance of diverse groups. The eventual inability of the cities to garner the vastly increased revenues needed to fuel this process helped bring the urban political process to a point of crisis. The fiscal crisis is indeed real—not because of mounting "needs" for services, but because of mounting demands for the benefits associated with the municipal bureaucracies. To block the responses of the bureaucracies to these demands for lack of revenues is to block a process of political accommodation in the largest population centers of the nation. The defection of the mayors was another sign of how deep the disturbances were, not in health agencies or welfare agencies, but in the urban political structure.

Federalism as a Constraining Influence

If mayors cannot resist the demands of contending groups in the cities, there are signs that the state and federal governments can, and will. The fiscal interrelations that undergird the federal system and leave the cities dependent on state and federal grants for an increasing portion of their funds are also a mechanism by which state and federal politics come to intervene in and control city politics. This is happening most clearly and directly through changes in state expenditures for the cities.

With their own taxing powers constricted from the outset, the mayors had little recourse but to turn to the states for enlarged grants-in-aid, trying to pass upward the political pressures they felt, usually summoning the press and the urban pressure groups for help. Since governors and legislators

were not entirely immune to pressures from the city constituencies, the urban states increased their aid to the big
cities.[49] Metropolises like New York City and Los Angeles now
get roughly a quarter of their revenues from the state.

Accordingly, state budgets also escalated, and state taxes
rose.[50] All in all, at least twenty-one states imposed new taxes
or increased old taxes in 1968, and thirty-seven states in 1969,
usually as a result of protracted struggle[51] North Carolina
enacted the largest program of new or increased taxes in its
history; Illinois and Maine introduced an income tax, bringing
to thirty-eight the number of states imposing some form of
income tax; South Carolina passed its first major tax increase
in a decade. Even Ohio moved to change its tradition of low
tax and low service policies that had forced thirteen school
districts in the state to close. Overall, state and local taxes

---

[49] By 1966–1967, per capita intergovernmental aid was substantially higher
for the central cities than suburban localities (contrary to popular impression). Per capita aid to Washington, D.C., was $181, compared to $81 in
the outlying suburbs; $174 to Baltimore, and $101 to the suburbs; $179 to
Boston, and $74 to the suburbs; $220 to New York City, and $163 to the
suburbs; $144 to Newark, and $53 to the suburbs; $70 to Philadelphia, and
$61 to the suburbs; $88 to Chicago, and $55 to the suburbs; $126 to Detroit,
and $115 to the suburbs (*State and Local Finances, op. cit.,* Table 29, p. 69).

[50] Arthur Levitt, Controller of the State of New York, recently released
figures showing that state spending had increased from $1.3 billion in
1956 to $3.9 billion in 1964, to an approximately $8 billion in 1968. In the
four years ending in 1968, state spending rose by an annual average of
$875 million, or 18.7 percent. In 1968 the spending increase was $1.4
billion, or 22.1 percent over the previous year (*The New York Times,* April
2, 1969–July 7, 1969). During this same five year period, state revenues
from taxes and federal aid increased from $3.7 billion to $7.2 billion. In
other words, spending exceeded revenues and by greater margins in each
of the successive years. The total deficit for the five year period amounted
to $2.5 billion, which, of course, had to be borrowed. A large part of this
rise in New York State's budget reflects aid to localities, which increased
from $622 million in fiscal 1955 to $1.04 billion in fiscal 1960, to $1.67
billion in 1965, and $3.23 billion in fiscal year 1969. State spending for aid
to education has doubled in the last six years, and the state share of
welfare and medicaid costs doubled in only four years.

[51] By 1971 the estimated difference between revenues and outlays were in
excess of $500 million in New York, California, and Texas. Florida was
short $120 million; New Jersey $100 million; Connecticut $200 million
(*The New York Times,* January 3, 1971). A handful of rural states, however,
were considering tax cuts.

rose from 5 percent of the Gross National Product in 1946 to more than 8 percent of the GNP in 1969. Americans paid an average of $380 in state and local taxes in the fiscal year 1968, $42 more per person than the previous year, and more than double the fiscal year 1967. The rate tended to be highest in urban states: In New York the per person tax burden was $576; in California, $540; in Massachusetts, $453. The low was in Arkansas, with a tax rate of $221.[52]

But raising taxes in Albany or Sacramento to pay for politics in New York City or Los Angeles is no simple matter, for the state capitals are not nearly as vulnerable as city halls to urban pressure groups, but are very vulnerable indeed to the suburbs and small towns that are antagonized by both higher taxes and city troubles. Besides, the mass of urban voters also resent taxes, especially when taxes are used to pay off the organized interests in the service systems, without yielding visibly better services.[53] Accordingly, even while taxes are raised, state grants to the cities are cut anyway. Thus, the New York State legislature reduced grant-in-aid formulas in

[52] Data provided by the Commerce Clearing House, as reported in *The New York Times,* September 27, 1970.

[53] A Gallup poll in 1969 showed that 49 percent would not vote for more money to pay for schools if additional taxes were sought, against 45 percent who would (*The New York Times,* August 17, 1969). Another key fact in understanding the populist character of the tax revolt is that state and local taxes consist mainly in sales and property taxes, and various user charges, all of which tend to be relatively regressive. Even the state income tax, when it is used, is usually imposed as a fixed percentage of income (unlike the graduated federal income tax, which takes more from those who have more, at least in principle). In any case, fully two-thirds of state revenues were raised from sales and gross receipt taxes. [*State and Government Finances in 1967,* U.S. Bureau of the Census (Washington, D.C.: Government Printing Office, 1968), Table I, p. 7]. Consequently the new taxes have had a severe impact on the working and middle classes, who are paying a larger and larger percentage of personal income to state and local government. In New York, state and local taxes now absorb over 13 percent of personal income; in California, over 12 percent; in Illinois and Ohio over 8 percent. As a result of rising state and local taxes (and price inflation), per capita real disposable personal income fell considerably between 1965 and 1969. See Paul M. Schwab, "Two Measures of Purchasing Power Contrasted," *Monthly Labor Review* (April 1971). By contrast, federal taxes declined as a percent of Gross National Product between 1948–1968, during which period state and local taxes rose from about 5 percent to 8 percent of GNP (*State and Local Finances, op. cit.,* Figure 5, p. 29). The "tax revolt" in the states should be no surprise.

welfare and medicaid (programs that go mainly to the central cities and mainly to blacks in those cities) in 1969[54] and again in 1971 (1970 was an election year and so the governor proposed increased aid to the cities without tax increases). Each time, the cuts were effected in all-night marathon sessions of the legislature, replete with dramatic denouncements by Democratic legislators from the cities and cries of betrayal from the mayors. Despite the cuts, anticipated state spending still rose by $878 million in 1969, the highest for any single year excepting the previous fiscal year in which the rise had been $890 million. By 1970 when the proposed budget had reached $8.45 billion, requiring $1.1 billion in new taxes, the outcry was so terrific that the governor reversed his proposals and led the legislature in a budget-slashing session, with welfare and medicaid programs the main targets.

When Governor Ronald Reagan, a self-proclaimed fiscal conservative, nevertheless submitted a record-breaking $6.37 billion budget for the 1969–1970 fiscal year, he met a storm of political protest that threatened a legislative impasse, leaving California without a budget. The next year Reagan proposed to solve the state's "fiscal crisis" by cutting welfare and medicaid expenditures by $800 million; even so, he submitted another record budget of $6.7 billion. When the long legislative battle that ensued was over, the governor signed an unbalanced budget of $7.3 billion, with substantial cuts in welfare and medicaid nevertheless.

Pennsylvania's former Republican Governor Raymond P. Shafer, in his short two years in office, managed to win the opposition of all but 23 percent of Pennsylvania voters as he and the legislature fought about how to raise $500 million in new revenues. At the beginning of his term in 1967, the governor was forced to raise state sales taxes to 6 percent, despite his campaign pledge of no new taxes, and early in 1969, with the budget $200 million short, he proposed that state's first income tax. When Shafer left office the income tax was enacted by his successor, Democratic Governor Milton Shapp, only to be voided by the Pennsylvania Supreme Court in 1971. A modified income tax law was finally passed, but by that time the state legislature was also making spend-

---

[54] Most of the 1969 welfare cuts were restored within a short time, but the 1971 cuts were not.

ing reductions, including a 50 percent cut in state education appropriations for ghetto districts.[55]

When Connecticut's 1969 biannual state budget proposal required a $700 million tax increase despite cuts in the welfare budget, the Democratic controlled General Assembly rebelled, forcing a hectic special session of the state legislature to hammer out a new budget and tax program. In the tumultuous weeks that followed, a compromise package presumably agreed upon by the Democratic governor and the Democratic majority in both houses was repeatedly thrown into doubt. When the session was over, Connecticut had passed the largest tax program in its history, had borrowed $32.5 million, and Governor John N. Dempsey had announced he would not seek reelection. Two years later Republican Governor Thomas J. Meskill engaged the legislature in battle again over another record budget that the governor proposed to pay for with a 7 percent sales tax—the highest in the country. Not only the legislature, but the insurance industries, the Mayor of Hartford, and 5,000 marchers took part in the protest that ensued, leading to a compromise tax package that replaced the sales tax increase with a new state income tax, together with more borrowing and new welfare cuts as well. A few short months later, after new public protests, the income tax was repealed, the sales tax increase was restored, and more spending cuts were made, mainly in state grants to municipalities and in welfare appropriations.

The New Jersey legislature, at a special session called by Democratic Governor Richard Hughes in 1969 to plead for added revenues for urban areas, rejected a new tax on banks and lending institutions—this despite the urging of the governor, who called the cities of the state "sick" and its largest city, Newark, "sick unto death," and despite the clamor of New Jersey's mayors. The legislature eventually agreed to redirect some existing urban aid funds to pay for increased police and fire salaries—a measure made particularly urgent after Newark's firemen went on strike, forcing the city to make emergency salary arrangements. When Republican Governor William T. Cahill took office later that year he signed a measure raising the New Jersey sales tax to 5 percent, claim-

---

[55] *The New York Times*, February 16, 1971; June 9, 17, 19, 25, 1971; and July 2, 1971.

ing he faced a "major state fiscal crisis" of a $300 million deficit.

Other state governments are locked in similar fiscal and political battles. Michigan began the 1972 fiscal year without authorization to spend money after the legislature had been virtually paralyzed by a six-months struggle over the $2 billion budget, which the governor had proposed to finance with a 38 percent increase in the state income tax. Wisconsin cut welfare and urban aid expenditures over Governor Ody J. Fish's protest and, having enacted a new and broadened sales tax, precipitated a march on the capital by Milwaukee poor. Not long afterward, Governor Fish resigned, imperiling the Wisconsin Republican party. In Rhode Island, Democratic Governor Frank E. Licht promised no new taxes in his reelection campaign in 1970 and two months later recommended an income tax, amidst loud voter protest. When Texas, having passed the largest tax bill in its history in 1969, faced a deficit of $400 million in 1971, Governor Preston E. Smith vetoed the entire second year of a two-year budget, which totaled $7.1 billion.

In brief, pressures from the big cities were channeled upward to the state capitals, with some response. At least in the big urbanized states, governors and legislatures moved toward bailing out the cities, with the result that state expenditures and state taxes skyrocketed. But the reaction is setting in; the taxpayers' revolt is being felt in state legislatures across the country. And as raucous legislative battles continue, a trend is emerging: The states are turning out to be a restraining influence on city politics, and especially on ghetto politics.

While in the main, grants-in-aid were not actually reduced, they were not increased enough to cover rising city costs either, and the toll is being taken. Some municipalities began to cut payroll and services. By 1971, vacancies were going unfilled in New York City, Baltimore, Denver, and Kansas City. San Diego and Cleveland reduced rubbish collection; Dallas cut capital improvements; Kansas City let its elm trees die.[56] Detroit started closing park toilets. And some city employees were actually being dismissed in Los Angeles, Cleveland,

[56] *The New York Times,* August 30, 1970; November 27, 1970; and May 25, 1971.

Detroit, Kansas City, Cincinnati, Indianapolis, Pittsburgh, and New York City. "This is the first time since the Depression that I have participated in this kind of cutback of education," said Cincinnati's Superintendent of Schools.[57] "You run as far as you can, but when you run out of gas you've got to stop," said Baltimore's Mayor Thomas J. D'Alesandro.

But the biggest cuts imposed by the states were in the programs from which blacks had gained the most as a result of their emergence as a force in the cities. Special state appropriations for health and education in ghetto districts were being cut; nine states cut back their medicaid programs;[58] and most important, at least nineteen states reduced welfare benefits by mid-1971, according to a *New York Times* survey. Moreover, new state measures to root out "welfare fraud," or to reinstitute residence restrictions, or to force recipients into work programs threatened far more drastic erosion of black gains in the near future.

There are signs that the federal government has also become a restraining influence on city politics. In the early 1960s, the national Democratic administration had used its grants to the cities to intervene in city politics, encouraging ghetto groups to demand more from city halls and forcing recalcitrant mayors to be more responsive to the enlarging and volatile ghettos, whose allegience had become critical to the national Democratic party. But a Republican administration was not nearly so oriented to the big cities, least of all to the ghettos of the big cities. Accordingly, the directions of the Great Society programs that the Nixon administration had inherited were shifted; bit by bit the new federal poverty agencies were scattered among the old-line federal bureaucracies, and the local agencies that had been set up in the ghettos were given to understand that confrontation tactics had to be halted. By now the Great Society looks much like traditional grant-in-aid programs; the federal fuel for ghetto agitation has been cut off. And new administration proposals for revenue sharing would give state and local governments firm control of the

---

[57] Nationally the annual rise in teacher salaries slumped to only 5.5 percent, after rising by about 8 percent each year for several years.

[58] Usually by limiting eligibility, or limiting the types of services covered, or requiring co-payments by patients. See *Health Law Newsletter* (Los Angeles: National Legal Program on Health Problems of the Poor, June 1971), p. 2.

use of federal grants, unhampered by the "maximum feasible participation" provisions that helped to stir ghetto demands in the 1960s.

There are other signs as well. The wage freeze stopped, at least temporarily, the escalation of municipal salaries, and this despite the outcry of teachers across the country. Finally, and perhaps most portentous for blacks, the administration's proposal for "welfare reform" would give the federal government a much larger role in welfare policy, lifting the struggle for who gets what outside of the arena of city politics where blacks had developed some power and had gotten some welfare.

Nor is it likely, were the Democrats to regain the presidency and thus regain the initiative in federal legislation, that the pattern of federal restraint would be entirely reversed. The conditions that made the ghettos a political force for a brief space of time seem to have changed. For one thing, there is not much action, either in the streets or in the voting booths. The protests and marches and riots have subsided, at least partly because the most aggressive people in the black population were absorbed; it was they who got the jobs and honorary positions yielded to blacks during the turmoil. These concessions, together with the Great Society programs that helped produce them, seem to have done their work, not only in restoring a degree of order to the streets, but in restoring ghetto voters to Democratic columns.

In any case, it was not ghetto insurgency of itself that gave blacks some political force in the 1960s. Rather it was that the insurgents were concentrated in the big cities, and the big cities played a very large role in Democratic politics. That also is changing; the cities are losing ground to the suburbs, even in Democratic calculations, and trouble in the cities is not likely to carry the same weight with Democratic presidents that it once did.

To be sure, a Democratic administration might be readier than a Republican one to refuel local services, to fund a grand new cornucopia of social programs. The pressures are mounting, and they come from several sources. One is the cities themselves, for to say that the cities are no longer as important as they once were is not to say Democratic leaders will want the cities to go under. Moreover, the inflated costs of the city are spreading to the suburbs and beyond, and these communities are also pressing for federal aid. Finally there is the force of the organized producers themselves, who have become very significant indeed in national politics; the education lobby and the health lobby already wield substantial influence in Washington, and they are growing rapidly. But while these pressures suggest that new federal funds will be forthcoming, the rise of the suburbs and the parallel rise of the professional lobbies indicate that it is these groups who are likely to be the main beneficiaries.

The future expansion of the federal role in local services has another, perhaps more profound, significance. It means that the decline of the local political unit in the American political structure, already far advanced, will continue. No matter how much talk we may hear about a "new American revolution," through which the federal government will return revenues and power to the people, enlarged federal grants mean enlarged federal power, for grants are a means of influencing local political developments, not only by benefiting some groups and not others, but through federally imposed conditions that come with the new monies. These conditions, by curbing the discretion of local political leaders, also erode the power of local pressure groups. As localities lose their political autonomy, the forces that remain viable will be those capable of exerting national political influence. Some may view this change as an advance, for in the past local communities have been notoriously oligarchical. But for blacks it is not an advance; it is in the local politics of the big cities that they have gained what influence they have.

The general truths to be drawn from this tale of the cities seem clear enough and familiar enough, for what happened in the 1960s has happened before in history. The lower classes made the trouble, and other groups made the gains. In the United States in the 1960s, it was urban blacks who made the trouble, and it was the organized producer groups in the cities who made the largest gains. Those of the working and middle classes who were not among the organized producers got little enough themselves, and they were made to pay with their tax monies for gains granted to others. Their resentments grew. Now, to appease them, the small gains that blacks did make in the course of the disturbances are being whittled away.

There is, I think, an even more important truth, though one

perhaps not so quickly recognized. These were the events of a political struggle, of groups pitted against each other and against officialdom. But every stage of that struggle was shaped and limited by the structures in which these groups were enmeshed. A local service apparatus, which at the outset benefited some and not others, set the stage for group struggle. Service structures that offered only certain kinds of benefits determined the agenda of group struggle. And a fiscal structure that limited the contest mainly to benefits paid for by state and local taxes largely succeeded in keeping the struggle confined within the lower and middle strata of American society. School teachers turned against the ghetto, taxpayers against both, but no one turned against the concentrations of individual and corporate wealth in America. Local government, in short, is important, less for the issues it decides, than for the issues it keeps submerged. Of the issues submerged by the events of the urban crisis, not the least is the more equitable distribution of wealth in America.